MASTERPIECES

A Dab at the Sixties and Seventies

Collected Journalism
1961–1981

John Wells

NEW ENGLISH LIBRARY

First published in Great Britain in 1982 by New English Library

First NEL Paperback Edition November 1983

NEL Books are published by
New English Library,
Mill Road, Dunton Green,
Sevenoaks, Kent.
Editorial office: 47 Bedford Square, London WC1B 3DP

Made and printed in Great Britain by Richard Clay
(The Chaucer Press) Ltd, Bungay, Suffolk

Wells, John
Masterpieces.
I. Title
828'.91407   PR6073.E4/

ISBN 0–450–05636–8

For Teresa, for Cecily, and for Dolly who wanted, more suitably, to call it *Monkeynuts*.

Contents

Acknowledgements

I should like to thank *The Spectator*, *The Observer*, *Punch*, *Vogue*, *The London Magazine*, *The Daily Telegraph Magazine*, *Harper's and Queen* and the BBC World Service for permission to reprint articles they originally commissioned. Also Georgia Tennant and Jenny Clifford for their help in preparing this selection.

A Word of Warning

If anyone is to blame for this collection appearing in print it is the Editor of *Private Eye*, Richard Ingrams. Having failed to get more than a limited trickle of jokes past his guard without the familiar roar of 'Nonsense, Wells!' or 'Rubbish!', I began in the early sixties to contribute would-be humorous pieces to other papers.

There being no response from Ingrams, I was emboldened to take over first the Press Column and then the Afterthought slot on *The Spectator*, where I began rather to fancy myself as a *belle-lettriste* and master of descriptive prose. I even got a letter from Graham Greene, correcting me on the use of a nominate clause. Then one morning I walked into the Coach and Horses, the *Private Eye* pub on the corner of Greek Street and Romilly Street, to find Ingrams reading aloud from my latest *Spectator* column to a group of chuckling toadies. He held his fingers splayed in the manner of a ham pantomime dame, and was reading in a high, fluting voice reminiscent of the late Godfrey Winn, lingering with eyelash-fluttering ecstasy over the purpler passages, and raising many a vulgar guffaw from the pimply fellows all about.

What distressed me, apart from the fact that the piece didn't stand up particularly well to the treatment, was that I was confronted with an image of myself with which I wasn't familiar. Warped in the distorting mirror of satire, I suddenly saw myself like some kind of effeminate *Doppelgänger*, mincing primly through the flowery fields in a mauve smock, shaking out my glossy locks as I dabbed the purple tints into my mannered little water-colours, and throwing up my hands in rapture at the loveliness

1

of the sky, the tiny birds that chirrup in the treetops.

In my own mirror, on the other hand, I had always seen myself as gripping a stump of battered cigar between yellowing teeth, a roguish gleam of self-irony in my eye, stabbing away with a tube of prussian blue in the manner of Kirk Douglas in the film about Van Gogh; wrestling with experience, mastering it, and slamming it down on the canvas in images of white-hot beauty lit with burning colour, pausing only occasionally to scratch the thick mat of hair on my chest and spit on the floor.

The next morning, I got a bright blue picture postcard from Switzerland. It was from Edward Mortimer, now a distinguished commentator on *The Times*, who had been a senior boy at Eton when I was teaching there. It was headed 'Come off it, Wells.' 'The Lake of Geneva,' it went on, 'looking curiously like a picture postcard of the Lake of Geneva, made a perfect setting for the twenty-ninth week of my *Spectator*-subsidised holiday. Stepping onto the speedboat, my water-skis on one arm and my second-best girl-friend on the other, I watched a few fleecy-white clouds scud out of sight behind the Jura. Some way away a small boy licked thoughtfully at an ice-cream, and in the distance I could discern the warbling of a grebe.' The piece that inspired the attack is called *The Silver Strand*, and can be found on page 202.

Oddly enough, being on the wrong end of the satirical tickling-stick did not have the effect it is meant to have in the textbooks. I was not cured or corrected. On the contrary it made me a great deal worse, more insensitive and even more extreme. Hence the present collection.

Leading as I do a rather fragmented life – the theatre critic of *The Times* when I was appearing as George Moore in *Jumpers* said I was not so much an embattled philosopher as a bewildered imp – it would be nice to say that on looking through twenty years' worth of yellowing print I had recognised certain essential themes, a pattern, that gave the book a structure. This has not been the case.

Instead I have divided it into a section on the Satire Boom (without which I would now probably be being regularly debagged as a beak at Eton and have taken to the bottle in a big way), a section on some of the people I've met and worked with, a section of humorous conceits, and a section given over to the hairy-chested Agony and Ecstasy alluded to above.

Malcolm Muggeridge, talking in an unguarded moment about the drawings of Feliks Topolski, once compared them to 'those images of Christ people believe they can descry in melting snow or the frost on a windowpane: if you look at all those lines long enough you can eventually convince yourself they bear some very vague resemblance to the subject'.

Looking at all the lines I've written at one time or another I have very much the same feeling. If I half-close my eyes and am in a reasonably generous mood I can just make out the original idea I had when I was trying to put it down on paper, but only just. I hope, as what they used to call in the eighteenth century 'the generous reader', you will approach the pages that follow with the same sympathy and short-sighted faith.

John Wells
1982

Smashing Idols 1

Not Filth But Satire

I have always been rather embarrassed as to what I should put in my passport under the heading of 'occupation'. I was particularly perplexed one wet Saturday in the summer of 1966, after the taxi had splashed through the puddles between the red sandstone gates of Keele, the University of North Staffordshire, along the tall avenue of beech trees, past the ponies in the paddock and through the half-finished buildings standing abandoned in the rain, to find myself billed as 'a satirist': 'A Satirist Speaks.' Apart from the tactful anonymity, reminiscent of those silhouetted interviews on television where 'A Drug-Addict Confesses' or 'A Transvestite Sings', I was worried by the implied exclamation mark. A satirist might be expected to produce vulgar sounds, pull faces, or imitate the distressingly painful walk of an elderly cabinet minister, but hardly to speak. Also the title seemed to suggest some sort of paradox: a destructive, irresponsible iconoclast indulging in a constructive, responsible, and even creative activity. I wandered gloomily about in the rain, having left London in hot sunshine and dressed for the beach in Clacton, and the water soaked into my shirt as I adjusted to the sober academic atmosphere.

Not that anyone else seemed to find the atmosphere in any way sober or oppressive. The weekend was officially devoted to the New Universities Festival, with delegates from seven other universities founded since the war, and with films, plays, seminars, debates and dances going on non-stop from dawn till the small hours, many of them at the same time. Lovely girls in short skirts ran about in the rain, hurrying from the third showing of *The War Game* to go and boo Mrs Mary Whitehouse at a seminar on responsible television. A little way up the hill some actors were standing in a small pit among heaps of wet, freshly dug clay, performing a play called *The Hole* to a small circle of enthusiasts in mackintoshes. Under the concrete lee of the Union building a group of folksingers were harmonising for the benefit of ABC Television, whose huge white and blue lorries stood about in the wet, surrounded by their cables and generators and crews. A Securicor man with a red face stood watching them. In another corner a photographer from the television company was arranging girls on pieces of sacking on a cold concrete seat, crawling about close to the ground and murmuring 'Just cross your legs, darling, we want a shot of your face mainly.'

Laid out in the rather cramped plan of a temporary army camp in the grounds of the old square-towered manor house, Keele, despite several good buildings, is still lacking in any real style. Set down at the middle of the university is a heavy grey-black brick church with a sharply sloping roof and two neo-Norman towers; a library just opposite that has been described as looking like a Mississippi steamboat, with a single slender clock-tower and decorated panels beneath its windows; and the Union building with its slightly heavy horizontal concrete slabs. In the rain the effect was depressing.

I also made the mistake of arriving in the refectory towards the end of lunch. The meat had a dark mature look, and the off-white balls of mashed potato fell heavily with the fibrous runner beans. The damsons floated in a particularly mouth-shrivelling red juice. Chewing the meat carefully I sat and looked despondently at the programme. 'A Satirist Speaks. The Physics Lecture Theatre.' Was this really the egalitarian Britain that *Beyond the Fringe* had laboured for three years to achieve? Was this the new deal we had implicitly campaigned for in the pages of *Private Eye*? I even became nostalgic for the medieval absurdities of Oxford. The vision of an innocent Conservative girl I had met two days before came back to me. 'If it hadn't been for your lot,' she had said, looking straight at me with her beautiful brown eyes, 'Macmillan would still be in charge and everything would be all right.' I drank my cup of fourpenny coffee and set off for the Physics Lecture Theatre.

To my surprise my entrance was greeted with a shout of laughter. I persisted nevertheless, giving a short outline of the Satirical Movement and defending our destructive iconoclastic attitude, taking as my text the dictum of Frankie Howerd, 'That's not filth, that's satire.' More laughter. I began to wonder if my flies were undone. I continued, illustrating my talk with examples of right-wing satire in which custard pies were slapped into the face of working-class clowns by constructive satirists who would then turn to the audience, pull their red noses off the extent of the elastic, and remark, 'But seriously folks, what a wonderful thing it would be for this great country of ours if British clowns could put up a roll of wallpaper without getting covered from head to foot in flour paste!' Gradually the audience settled down and became more serious. A girl at the front in a low-cut summer dress fell asleep. I dwelt on the beneficial effects of iconoclasm in destroying hardened and meaningless social conventions. I quoted Peter Simple of the *Daily Telegraph*. Those still awake seemed impressed. By the end of an hour they appeared to be convinced that satire was no laughing matter.

Satisfied, I walked back through the university gardens. The rain had stopped, the birds were singing, and there was a heavy scent of rhododendrons in the air. The sky was a soft blue, the clouds on the horizon a pale yellow. The lights began to come on in the low modern buildings against the dark curve of the hill and the cattle stood out in silhouette on the skyline. From the Union came the deep reverberating beat of an amplified bass, and a Scottish country dancing group whooped to a reel in a white hut under the trees. Suddenly it seemed that my scheme to raze Oxford to the ground, so that you could stand at Carfax and look down the gentle grassy slope towards Magdalen and see the Oxen up to their bellies in the Ford by the Botanical Gardens, and then rebuild it as the University of South Oxfordshire, might after all be worthwhile. I can already see the headlines: 'A Satirist Acts.'

Satire, like tragedy, the marble nude and military government, was officially invented by the Greeks. Archilocus, who lived on the island of Paros in the seventh century BC, was the son of a priest and a slave girl. Because of his mother's lowly birth his future father-in-law, apparently at the last moment, cancelled the marriage. As a result Archilocus composed terrible and angry verses against his father-in-law, who hanged himself, as did his intended bride.

In fact, satire had obviously been going on for a great deal longer than that: probably since one of our first ancestors curled his long hairy ape-like lip to sneer at another of our first ancestors and imitated his ungainly simian lope. But Satirists presumably prefer the idea of Archilocus inventing it because his was a success story. He was irritated, thought of a brilliantly witty and terrible reply, and his enemies dropped dead.

Ever since then Satire, as well as trying to be brilliantly witty and terrible, has always been credited with the same power of magic, like a curse, that can cause those attacked to shrivel up and disappear. Like the witch or the magician, the satirist imitates his victim, makes little puppets of his victim, pictures of his victim, imagines him speaking, waking and sleeping, and tries, by exaggerating his faults, to destroy him.

However, as Jonathan Swift discovered, during the great period of English satire in the early eighteenth century which produced the four brilliantly sustained, intellectually controlled books of *Gulliver's Travels*, the perfectly balanced verse of Alexander Pope and the theatrical genius of *The Beggar's Opera* by John Gay, causing your enemies to drop dead is not as easy as that. After the ridicule of lawyers in *Gulliver's Travels*, Swift makes Lemuel Gulliver complain in the preface to the Second Edition that he expected to see bonfires of law books all down the Strand. Instead he found the lawyers more powerful and more prosperous than ever, and everyone from little children to old ladies, and presumably the lawyers themselves, all roaring with laughter at the book.

This, for some reason always seems to be the satirist's doom. He mimics his victim, sticks verbal pins into him, the crowd, he hopes, roar with laughter, but somehow the victim fails to drop dead. On the contrary the crowd, by the end of the performance, seem to find the victim rather more endearing than they did at the beginning.

After all the mockery, abuse and slander it has heaped on the Press and the BBC, *Private Eye*'s tenth birthday was marked with flattering feature articles in all the papers, there was a nostalgic programme of homage on BBC television and Richard Ingrams was invited to dinner at Ten Downing Street.

Private Eye, admittedly, got off to a bad start. It was launched at a time, in 1961, when the revue *Beyond the Fringe* was running in the West End, and *That Was The Week That Was* was beginning on television, when SATIRE in big neon letters had just struck London with the force of a major craze. Since then there have been mini-skirts, bell-bottomed trousers, hamburgers and Che Guevara moustaches, but then it was Satire. There was also a nightclub, run by roughly the same gang, advertised as 'London's First Satirical Nightclub', and called The Establishment.

Beyond the Fringe is now theatrical history, *That Was The Week* slumbers in the vaults of Television Centre, preserved on videotape, The Establishment is now a gambling club. But *Private Eye* survives.

On the balance of probabilities, it shouldn't have done. Several major libel suits have cost it tens of thousands of pounds, but, perversely, these have only strengthened it: film stars and television personalities have flocked to organise charity shows for the magazine, and so bail it out.

But the secret of its massively prosperous failure is probably due less to Satire than to the very limited size of the team who started and maintained it, and to the organic continuity of its style and appearance, the same now as it was when *Private Eye* was a yellow-paper experiment of 150 copies stapled together by hand by debutante volunteers in William Rushton's bedroom in Scarsdale Villas, Kensington.

The core of its regular staff were all at school together, at Shrewsbury, and ran the school magazine, *The Salopian*. Politically, it has always been a paper of prejudice: Paul

Foot, who stayed with it for the first ten years and established its reputation as a newspaper rather than a humorous review in print, is a devout Trotskyite, and Ingrams a devoutish old-fashioned patrician Christian Tory who is hugely amused by foreigners, women, homosexuals, the Monarchy, the middle class, the working class and Trotskyites like Foot. It is perhaps an object lesson in English tolerance that they put up with each other for so long. The fact that the country as a whole has put up with *Private Eye* is proof not only of English tolerance: it is an example of the English ruling classes' capacity for absorbing new and irritating elements in a way that eventually makes the irritating elements part of themselves and hence harmless. But that may just be the inevitable lot of the satirist.

Thinking again about Archilocus, I am convinced his prospective wife and father never hanged themselves at all. I think it's more likely that they roared with laughter, called him a clever little man, and all lived happily ever after.

According to the myth-makers, most of whom were not present at the time, British Satire was born in Edinburgh on the stage of the Lyceum Theatre on a warm summer night in 1960.

In fact, when *Beyond the Fringe* opened there was very little new material in it. The opening sketch, in which a tiny Russian pianist was taught to say 'Mr Khrushchev (raspberry) Mr Macmillan (sound of beaming approval)' rather than the other way round, was new, and set the atmosphere for the evening, but the majority of the pieces that followed had been well tried out by Dudley Moore and Alan Bennett in Oxford, and by Peter Cook and Jonathan Miller in Cambridge, and even in London. What they did, by bringing together a lot of individual cabaret acts in one show was to smash up the old revue formula, and also to use what had been a medium for communicating pink twaddle into an outlet for reasonably intelligent ideas.

Until then the majority of revues had followed roughly the same pattern. Directors literally insisted on the cast cleaning their teeth immediately before they went on, and there was a good deal of grinning and dancing about: there were sketches and songs about Night Starvation and the Income Tax.

The *Beyond the Fringe* team did not beam ingratiatingly at the audience. They hardly danced at all. The fact that in the suggestion of a dance they did during the War Sketch Peter Cook was still out of step after the show had been running for two years, may conceivably have had something to do with it, but on reflection it was quite logical. If you wanted to amuse your friends after dinner in 1960 you did not on the whole leap about singing songs about the Income Tax.

But the bird-brained intellectuals still insisted on discussing not so much the virtues of the performers as the degree to which the performers had fulfilled their own secret fantasies. Here at last, they shrilled, was Left-Wing Satire. If, they mused, an upper-class drunk had from time to time teetered on to the music-hall stage, it was always made clear by Right-Wing Satirists that he was not in a position of power. He was not, for instance, a Cabinet Minister. Now here at last Mr Macmillan was being brutally satirised up there for not being able to find Europe on the globe. Hurrah, hurrah for the Revolution, and with the strains of the Red Flag ringing in their ears they strode powerfully out the theatre to attack the Lobster Thermidor. Right-wing critics like Harold Hobson were left with the cold comfort of having seen Peter Cook's retired coal-miner, in one surreptitious Right-wing sketch, revealed and savagely satirised as a daft old nit.

So carried away were they, indeed, by this potent political satire that many of them were put in mind of Berlin in the thirties. They did not appear to have noticed that the most committed sketches, like the Death Cell scene, or Alan Bennett's Reasonable Man on South Africa, were the least successful with the audience. It was still Berlin in the thirties. Nostalgic for the clear-cut issues of fascism, they dreamed of a smoke-filled cellar, Bertolt Brecht mournfully playing an accordion in one corner and some grim-faced gagman in the spotlight out front, rising from the waves of thoughtful laughter to plant barb after

11

barb in the rump of the Nazi Beast. And outside the fascist jackboots rang on the cobbles.

The myth had certainly caught on sufficiently in the late summer of 1961 to be the subject of much ribaldry and obscene abuse among the cast in what had been a strip club in Greek Street, and was now being redesigned by Sean Kenny as The Establishment. This, according to the myth, grew naturally and directly out of *Beyond the Fringe*. In fact it had been thought of by Peter Cook in Cambridge a year before *Beyond the Fringe* began.

It was intended simply to be somewhere to go in the middle of London where you could get a drink or a meal and watch a show without spending too much money. As the show was to be written by John Bird and Peter Cook it would admittedly have had something of the same style, myth or no myth. What the myth did was to fill the subscription lists for the club and they made £6,000 from that source alone even before it opened. If this had the effect of unsettling the business judgment of Nicholas Luard, Cook's business partner in the club, then the myth could be said to have been responsible for its collapse. Someone, certainly, and it seems unlikely that it was Cook, believed in the value of the fashion sufficiently to have an illuminated sign fixed outside the club: 'London's First Satirical Nightclub.'

To the disciple of the Berlin-in-the-Thirties cult nothing could have been more dramatically exciting than the opening night. The sign up outside, the harsh wooden decor, the clusters of exposed spotlights, the little stage, the wooden tables, the committed cast running through their lines for the last time. The only thing that was missing, it seemed, was the harsh clatter of the fascist jackboots. But the cast had every reason to wince when the sound of boots did finally reach their expectant ears with the creak of the elastic-sided variety affected at that time by the stripe-shirted jet set.

The chaos was indescribable. Television arc-lights blazed above the crush, girls in expensive dresses wriggled and squealed in the crowd, their rock-jawed escorts bellowing above the din. 'Hello, Jeremy! You going to Antonia's thrash on Thursday?' Satire was in, and they

12

were damned if they were going to miss a second of it. Admittedly it meant rubbing shoulders with some pretty weird beatnicky sort of people, the food was second-rate, and one had to sit through hours of the most awful political stuff. Somewhere in a corner, far away above the heads of the crowd, vainly trying to compete with the roar of conversation, the actors moved through their entertainment. I came on, shortly after midnight, to perform a Left-wing impersonation of John Betjeman and they were still in no mood to leave.

For a short time it seemed as if everything was going to be all right. The club settled down to what it had been intended to be: there was a reasonably good and cheap lunch, good films in the afternoons, a picture gallery in the bar on the first floor, and in the evening the show upstairs and Dudley Moore played jazz in the cellar. With John Bird, John Fortune and Eleanor Bron the shows were popular and well attended and most of the fashionable lunatics seemed to have disappeared. Then drunks came reeling in from Greek Street, there were bottle fights, the staff turned out to be fiddling the management blind, and when Peter Cook went to America in 1963 the club, financially stretched as it was with ventures like the unsuccessful showbiz magazine *Scene*, finally collapsed.

The entertainment at The Establishment differed from *Beyond the Fringe* largely in that it contained film, occasional little situation pieces of the type later performed by John Fortune and Eleanor Bron on television – girl and boy find it difficult to communicate, man's difficulties in approaching a doctor he is slightly acquainted with and asking him to perform an abortion – and also a certain amount of probing into religious and sexual areas normally swathed in silence.

Meanwhile, within a month of The Establishment opening, the myth-makers had pounced on the first number of *Private Eye*. The first issue had a photograph of the Albert Memorial on the cover. Albert himself was seen in silhouette, sitting in pensive mood beneath the spire of the monument. 'Britain's Spaceman Albert Gristle,' the caption read, 'awaits blastoff.'

This was too much for the myth-makers. Here was the

13

grand, unselfconscious, satirical movement entering journalism: clearly a development of The Establishment. They had missed two things. First, the little drawing of Queen Victoria who stood looking up at Albert. 'Ho, ho,' she was saying, 'very satirical.' And secondly, that *Private Eye* was nothing at all to do with The Establishment.

The first title suggested for the new magazine was *Bladder*. Eventually this was rejected for personal reasons: Rushton's grandmother was lying ill upstairs with a bladder complaint, and it was felt that the name might be thought to be in bad taste. This is only interesting in that it is probably the only time that considerations of taste have in any way influenced the editorial line of the magazine.

Eventually, on a capital of £350, *Private Eye* was brought out, and, after establishing itself, looked for a backer and was bought by Peter Cook. But there was certainly no question of link-up between the magazine and the club. Both groups eyed each other with the greatest suspicion. Hilarious attempts were made from time to time, doubtless in the spirit of satire, to unite us. What came to be known contemptuously as 'Satirical Lunches' were organised by Nicholas Luard in The Establishment. The two factions sat on opposite sides of the room, crouching on low stools, and eating as best they could off even lower tables in front of them served by small Greek waiters. The Establishment cast sneered across at us, despising us either because we wore waistcoats or, in Ingrams' case because he kept his trousers up with string, which they considered 'eccentric'. We sneered back at them, though I can't quite remember why.

The ultimate expression of the Boom was the series that began with *That Was The Week That Was*, and went on to *Not So Much a Programme*, *BBC 3* and the *Late Show*. Whereas the other three satirical phenomena had been organic developments, these programmes, in the absence of Peter Cook and John Bird who had by now taken their own shows to America, were initially created by bringing together very disparate talents who had not worked together before, led by ex-Cambridge whizz-kid D. Frost who had been discovered by the BBC's Ned Sherrin working in cabaret at the Blue Angel. Rushton appeared in it too, Ingrams and Christopher Booker contributed sketches, but they were working with a great many journalists and actors of a more traditional showbiz background. The demand for the programmes was quite clearly created by the myth, and they suffered equally from an inorganic rootlessness and a weakness for following the current fashion. When the programmes began, the impact on viewers who had not seen manifestations of this kind before was clearly very great: the fact that they appeared on the BBC made them stunning.

Again, as in *Beyond the Fringe*, the basic innovation was that people were talking in the same way when the cameras were on them as they did when the cameras were not.

There was certainly very little that was satirical about *Not So Much a Programme*, despite its origins. Like its predecessor, it was basically an educational programme. Gerald Kaufman and others offered 'good conversation'. The fact that it made jokes about politicians, the fact that actors occasionally stumbled before the cameras using such words as 'bum' and 'po', was really only sugar on the pill. The real dose could be discovered in the opening lyric, written by Miss Caryl Brahms, a slightly earnest and rather sentimental humorist of the old school. 'Not so much a programme, more a way of life,' it ran, 'or a way of looking at the world. One eye open wide, one eye closed: and between the two the picture gets composed.' The viewer in other words was exhorted to come in and share the sophisticated view of things. One eye open for what Alan Bennett's clergyman calls 'all the good things of life', and one eye closed in a knowing wink: faith in cynicism. Nevertheless *Not So Much a Programme* ran, incredibly, three nights a week for twenty-six weeks, and by the time *BBC 3* and the *Late Show* came along the material was stretched very thin indeed and the public had had enough.

The really interesting story, of course, is of the supreme influence of Peter Cook. Visitors to Cambridge when he was there found whole dramatic societies imitating him. John Bird and John Cleese both acknowledge a debt. David Frost, whose complexion then was not as perfect as it is today, borrowed so heavily that Cook called him the Bubonic Plagiarist. At *Private Eye* in the sixties we pinched his jokes and imitated his style so closely that people believed he had written it. Indeed it could be argued there was no such thing as Satire, only Cook.

'His vitality was his finest characteristic. He had only to enter a lecture hall full of hundreds of noisy students, or a room, or a stage, with his special walk, his sharply cut bronze skull slightly tilted and thrust forward, and there was silence. . . . There he stood, ugly, brutal, dangerous, with close-cropped red hair, his hands in his trouser pockets, and one felt that the devil himself couldn't shift him. . . . It was the man's intense aliveness, the energy which allowed him to defy sniggering ridicule and proclaim his brazen hymn to humanity.'

Not, as you might think, a convert's description of his youth leader entering an early meeting of the Nazi Party, but an obituary for Frank Wedekind, author of the *Lulu* plays and *Spring Awakening*, written in 1918 by Bertolt Brecht. Both of them were cabaret performers, and the lines, written by one professional about another, describe the art-form very accurately.

What impressed me, in the late fifties, about the cabaret in Berlin, in Hamburg, and in Munich where I was then living, was the absolutely un-English seriousness of the institution. It is easy to talk in rather abstract terms about the breaking down of the fourth wall of the stage, the involvement of the audience, and the cabaret performer's direct address to the people listening to him. That is all true, but Sandy Powell – 'Can you hear me, Mother?' – was doing the same thing on the end of the pier at Eastbourne when I was taken there as a child.

What was new was the tables, waitresses discreetly slipping under the spotlight to bring beer and sausages, the experience of never being much more than a few feet away from the performers, the dramatisation of ideas normally reserved for newspaper cartoons, and above all the complicity and social consciousness of the audience, in which the performers swam, basked and glittered like fish in sunlit water.

The social consciousness was not on a very high level in

terms of information: familiarity with the small print rather than the headlines of a daily newspaper was probably as much as it amounted to, but there was sharp awareness that life was not just a static experience, as in the Television Light Entertainment view of the world, where we have all been given an anus and a mother-in-law, over which we can chuckle in cosy mutual reassurance. German cabaret audiences accepted and laughed at the fact that for every operation there is an operator, and for every mug a mugger. Whether, over the years, it has done them any good is another question.

What was also apparent was that they were there because they not only admired the performers' comedic gifts, but shared their view of how society was manipulated. They were not, as the barbed-shaft school of criticism would have us believe, beef mountains of the bourgeoisie, bent on impaling themselves on the artist-executioner's knife in the manner of Lord Longford entering a Copenhagen sex club, but normal seekers of entertainment who liked it straight and were prepared to pay for it. The tradition existed. For people of that particular turn of mind, who in England would have been otherwise engaged, it was as familiar a place to go and spend their money and the evening as the theatre or the cinema. But at the centre of the particular form of entertainment was the magnetism and wit of the performer, and his ability to juggle, with the tacit consent of a small and intimate audience, with their shared prejudices and beliefs.

Like any other medium dealing in ideas, the German cabaret showed its political skills best when it was under attack, either from heckling drunks or Government censorship, as long as the majority of the audience remained in sympathy. And unless the whole house was bought out at the box office by enemies wishing to indulge in some kind of expensive gallic prank to humiliate the cast, rather than simply closing the club, it is logical that only those still in sympathy would pay for tickets.

Werner Finck, reminiscing after the Second World War, remembers working at the Katakombe in Berlin in 1935, where the performers were all Aryan. When a Nazi heckler

17

called him a dirty Jew, he replied to the effect that he was sorry, the Nazi was mistaken, he only *looked* that intelligent.

Instances of real heroism in the face of totalitarian government certainly existed in the cabaret, just as they did in newspapers, nursing or basket-weaving. Such clubs were unquestionably rallying points of resistance, like some pubs and some churches. But the line that has the most convincing ring to it, as truly a political remark as Brecht's on Wedekind, is that of Tristan Tzara: exulting in the wings in Paris in the twenties as the audience went mad after his *Vaseline Symphony* – a work for twenty players I would give a great deal to have seen – he shouted 'It's exactly like the Communist meetings in Berlin!' In other words, he had successfully worked the room, and the political relationship between performers and audience was, from Tzara's point of view, entirely satisfactory.

By 1961 I had worked in late-night revues two years running at the Edinburgh Festival, both of which were in the style of small-print observation and occasional sentimentality that I had seen in Germany, and the second show was actually recognised as being in that tradition by the *Süddeutsche Zeitung*.

Watching Peter Cook, who had also visited a lot of German satirical and other nightclubs in the late fifties, as he supervised the carpenters converting the Establishment Club before it opened in October, I was convinced that Cabaret could be transplanted into England.

The club opened, and was unquestionably the genuine article. If the form of entertainment – the drinks, waiters ducking under the spotlights, etc – had been more familiar to the English business mind, things might have been very different. As it was the political mismanagement lampooned outside was ironically matched inside, and eighteen cases of Scotch were reported to have vanished from the bar in the first three months.

The political relationship with the audience was certainly established, though 'Satire' was welcomed as something novel, English, and terribly clever, rather than being part of an old European tradition. If some regular replacement had been found when the original company, John Bird,

John Fortune and Eleanor Bron, went to America, it is possible it could have survived rather than becoming a gambling club.

Students of Kabarett would also have recognised similarities to the genre in *That Was The Week That Was* and its sequels. *Grossièrement maquillé*, as the official French protest termed it, I could, with a few extra twitches of the eyebrows and a prolonged tremble in the voice, coax the audience into sharing a few generalised prejudices against General de Gaulle. But whatever our shortcomings as writers or performers in failing to dominate and hold the audience of 12,000,000 to which the show built up in the first few weeks, the reason for its withering away was ultimately a lack of roots in the English tradition.

Ned Sherrin, the producer, a University-educated showman of considerable extravagance, more interested on the whole in camp song and dance routines than in the structure of government, managed to create his own department, somewhere between Current Affairs and Light Entertainment. His successor, Hugh Burnett, came from Documentaries, and the BBC's doubts about where we actually belonged were reflected in the blank stares of the dear old ladies sent to us at random by the BBC Ticket Unit to provide us with an audience, when they would obviously have preferred to have been watching a recording of *Dixon of Dock Green*.

This lack of an organic home for satirical cabaret was dramatised very vividly for me some years later, when I went to do a one-man show at a University Dance, and due to some confusion about rooms, actually had to lead a group of relentless satire enthusiasts past the alternative entertainment, a Punch and Judy show and a traditional jazz band, both accommodated in a corner of the marquee, to the necessary quiet of a lecture hall.

We have a great many cabaret performers rivalling Wedekind in their ability to silence a room and entertain their audiences. Spike Milligan has the same daemonic energy, Barry Humphries can tease and flatter an audience with a genius for solidly rehearsed precision and brilliant improvisational polish that will send historians, with only the scripts to go on, into frenzies of the barbed-shaft-

19

thudding-into-the-soft-underbelly-of-the-complacent-bourgeoisie style of writing.

Much lunchtime, pub, documentary and politically committed theatre springs from the cabaret tradition. The accuracy of a mimic like Mike Yarwood succeeds absolutely at headline level. Singers in conventional nightclubs still struggle to overcome the babble and clatter from the tables. Specialist clubs like Ronnie Scott's play to attentive audiences, and strip clubs playing to equally attentive audiences continue to multiply. But the smoke-filled cellar, the politically viable, economically sound and publicly accepted container full of sunlit, subtly shifting sympathy where the fish can flash and gambol in their own element has either passed us by or is yet to be created.

Smashing Idols 2

Alberts All

There is a natural sympathy that exists between people who have been through a disaster together, however marginal their involvement, and whatever happens to them afterwards. The same is true of a success. And whatever else it was or wasn't, the so-called Satire Boom of the early sixties, for entertainers of a subversive disposition, was a period of unprecedented success.

Not that the sympathy was necessarily apparent at the time. At the height of the Satire Boom, Peter Cook engaged the Alberts and Bruce Lacey, a trio of eccentric musical clowns whose specialities included bubble-blowing automata and exploding camels, to appear on Monday evenings at The Establishment Club in Greek Street. John Bird recalls the Alberts being greeted by the intellectual commentators as 'a kind of brilliant excrescence on the satire wave, capable of doing wonderfully liberated things they couldn't expect from the serious nose-to-the-grindstone satirists', and remembers having to pick a way through the Alberts' junk to get to the stage. John Fortune, on one occasion, pushed a stuffed camel out of the way to get down the stairs and inadvertently set off a maroon which deafened him in the enclosed space and left him unable to hear a single cue for the rest of the evening.

Shortly afterwards they appeared in their most successful show ever in the West End, *An Evening of British Rubbish*, with the Scots poet Ivor Cutler. Bernard Levin, one of the critics who was most enthusiastic about it, claimed that they had struck a vein of surrealism even purer than that of more disciplined performers like Bentine and Milligan. Certainly *An Evening of British*

Rubbish, apart from its inspired comedy, was an unforgettable evening in the theatre. Moth-eaten men in beards and baggy Edwardian clothes strode on and off the stage, there were a great many apparently random bangs and explosions, trumpets were blown, jokes were muttered and shouted, usually into the wings, the stuffed camel had its tail turned like a starting handle to the accompaniment of further bangs, more dirty men in ancient military uniforms strode on and off shouting at each other, someone appeared dressed as a bee, a mechanical dummy was wheeled on to deliver a monosyllabic political speech, a musician in a grubby white tie and tails attempted to play the 'cello, and subversive figures winking at the audience and slyly tapping their noses were seen to lay a charge of dynamite under his chair, reel out the cable to a plunger, and finally blow themselves up with another thunderous bang.

Lenny Bruce, who had seen their act at The Establishment, was incoherent with enthusiasm, threatened to put them under contract for life, and engaged them to appear in New York. When they arrived he was in prison.

But the Alberts and Bruce Lacey were launched a long time before they were swept to international success on the high tide of Satire. They claim, with some justification, to have been twenty years ahead of their time in pioneering light shows, happenings and what would now pass for a fashionably inventive style of dressing. As Bruce Lacey says: 'In those days, we were bizarre figures.'

I first saw them in the mid-fifties when I was still at school, listening to the Goons on the wireless, and wincing with an embarrassment I can still feel as our first-ever jazz band broke the silence of Big School at Eastbourne College with an appalling rendering of 'When the saints go marching in'. The Alberts were playing at Humphrey Lyttleton's Jazz Club in Oxford Street, an ear-splitting duet for miniature trombone and miniature trumpet, and although Humph was at that time the hero, and George Melly did a dance, they remain the only clear memory I have of the evening.

The Alberts in real life, to the extent that it differs at all from their life on the stage, are Tony and Douglas Gray.

22

They originally took their father's name, Albert, in order to make exactly that distinction, and they have always kept it. They came from a musical family, although neither of their parents were professional musicians, and both spent their National Service, shortly after the end of the war, in Egypt. Douglas, who has since collected as many old cars as he has old musical instruments, and actually owns a Swiss charabanc that he drove back himself over the Alps, was driving an Egyptian bus in Alexandria, and Tony, ironically for someone who says he doesn't like being thought of as a junk man, spent his time salvaging burned-out tanks in the Western Desert.

Bruce Lacey began as a child in a tap-dancing troupe, and passed out of the Royal College of Art with a first-class diploma, a silver medal and a travelling scholarship. He recently summoned a committee of students at the Royal College to sniff his fur coat after the Senior Common Room had told him it smelt, and he obviously enjoys telling the story about a gallery owner who returned to this country to find his premises being used for a Bruce Lacey exhibition and 'refused to set foot in the building until all this rubbish had been cleaned out'.

The use of the word rubbish to describe their own work is significant: when they use it, it means British rubbish, a modestly dismissive description of their unpretentious artistic achievement. It also plays into the hands of hostile critics and managers not disposed to promote or encourage them, who call it lack of professionalism, and actually miss the point.

In terms of punctuality and turning up for an engagement at the right place on the right day they are as professional as anyone else. The first sign of their arrival is a convoy of ancient vehicles parked outside, and a heap of old costumes, mostly military, and the familiar cumbersome junk piled up in the middle of the dressing room floor. Again it's all right for them to call it junk, but if anyone else does they are liable to get a lecture on the considerable value of each piece. Tony Gray, a skinny, rather nervous man with pale blue eyes, a straggly beard and a red corduroy cap, lopes about smoking a long cigar, and looking like an eccentric German yachting enthusiast

23

before the First World War. Douglas stands still, enjoying the chaos mounting all around him, plump and twinkling with round gold-rimmed spectacles and a broad-brimmed hat, a pipe, and thick, broad-checked tweeds in the manner of G. K. Chesterton. In both cases they give the impression of being costumes, interchangeable with any from the heap on the floor.

Bruce Lacey is a more workmanlike figure, Victorian rather than Edwardian, with a deeply furrowed face, black side-whiskers, a blue chin and deep black fingernails. There are also a great many hangers-on, friends, wives and children, all of whom are dressed as if from a dressing-up box with vague nineteenth-century nostalgia.

On stage the inspired amateurishness comes face to face with an ancient tradition of lifeless professionalism. With an audience of friends and enthusiasts they are unbeatable, and the energy of the jokes they create on their side of the proscenium arch is extremely powerful. With a commercial audience it often seems as though all the energy is short-circuiting itself. Punch lines appear to be muffed or fumbled, nobody ever seems to come in on cue, and the almost constant shouting and blowing of instruments create a self-contained atmosphere on the stage, reminiscent of a children's playground or group therapy at a progressive lunatic asylum.

For all their doggedly amateur contempt for the audience, their professional devotion to duty is heroic. Bruce Lacey's experience was typical, when he was engaged to entertain a Concrete Congress in Nottingham. 'It's truth we're after on the stage, you see, spontaneity. I was on my own that time, trying to do a job on the quiet without the Alberts to make a bit more money, and I stopped doing the act after a bit and started talking about my wife and family. And they started slow handclapping, you see. All these people in evening dress and bow ties. So I said alright, let's have a show of hands, those who want me to stop. And out of eight hundred, seven hundred and ninety said get off. So I went off and put on this little Japanese costume, and as it was a Concrete Congress I'd been told not to mention the word brick. So I brought this brick on, and they all booed. Then I put it across the top of these two chairs and did a karate chop and broke it, and they all cheered. Then I put a piece of concrete there instead, and did the same thing, and my hand broke off. I had this wooden hand, you see. So in the end it was a great success. And I was talking to one of the people afterwards who'd voted for me to stay on, and he said "Have you ever been on the stage before?", and I said "Yes, since the age of nine".'

Trying to define what they set out to achieve on the stage, Bruce Lacey is hesitant to commit himself to anything that sounds too pretentious. 'I suppose you could say that what we're trying to do is to show the family reality, and include our own fantasies. I always want to be the mad inventor who can draw a women to him with this mysterious magnetism that I feel I haven't got myself, Tony's always had his Errol Flynn complex, and Douglas wants to be a Russian landlord.'

What is the theatre's loss is that they don't seem to need the professional stage in order to fulfil their fantasies. Bruce Lacey is already a successful mad inventor, recently remarried to an attractive young wife, Tony Gray is something of an Errol Flynn, and Douglas and he are both English country squires, if not Russian landlords.

They support themselves, thanks to their early apprenticeship in the printing trade and their resulting qualification for allied union membership, by driving newspaper delivery vans for two nights a week. The work is sufficiently well paid to let them live quietly for the rest of the time in old vicarages in the country. It's a difficult job to get, and as Tony himself says, it's not one that appeals to everybody. 'They might say "The train's gone to Cardiff" and you say "Cardiff?" and three hours later you're there. I mean all you brilliant journalists and writers, but it all ends up in the back of a newspaper lorry. It's the end product that counts, it's still got to get to the readers. So I suppose we are cosseted a bit, like Spitfire pilots.' Douglas sees it in less romantic terms, 'Half a ton of newspapers to shift. Cor! Not surprising I'm tired when I get home, I can tell you.'

In the driver's cab of the blue-painted double-decker

Leyland bus that he has converted into his London *pied à terre* on wheels, Tony Gray, now in his late forties, has obviously lost none of his old skill in handling big vehicles. A big cigar in his mouth and wearing a well-cut white linen suit, he hauls the steering wheel round and sets course down Constitution Hill, solid and serene above the shiny tops of the taxis.

'It was the first thing I ever did really well, driving a tank. I volunteered, you see, so I could choose what mob I went into. It wasn't like being in the infantry: you could take such a lot with you – overcoats, crates of this and that – I suppose that's what may have given me the idea for the bus. When I came out of the army I think my main ambition was to be independent, go where I liked. That was where the clothes were important: I always used to wear a black velvet jacket, a white shirt and a black bow tie and that way I soon found that I could get in anywhere any time.

'I think what I wanted to do after the war was to live like they did in the old days. Not bother about passports. Be a citizen of Salisbury, or wherever you happened to live, with letters of recommendation and so on. I've never liked time much: I think I was happiest in Spitsbergen where it was always two o'clock in the morning. Same with money. Never liked that either. I suppose what I wanted was to be a man whose word was his bond. Be a gentleman really.'

It was their work in the theatre which led Tony to the idea of the bus. 'Landladies wouldn't have us, you see. No children, no dogs, all that. So I thought of this. Park it outside the stage door and we could all sleep in it. Somewhere you could entertain people like Lionel Bart.

'First one we got offered for nothing by a vicar. It was parked in a field and the farmer was ploughing round it. Someone had smashed the top in driving under a low bridge, all the glass was broken. We drove it home though, half way across England. Gave the woman at a filling station a bit of a scare. Douglas was driving, wearing one of his German uniforms. She said "Who are you?" I said "We're married. Sometimes he's the conductor and sometimes I am."

'This one used to be an old school bus. Does about

fifteen miles to the gallon on diesel. The man who owned it said it was getting too small. He wanted two hundred for it, so I said "I'll take it. Do you want a deposit?" He said "No, I'll see you," so I drove it off and gave him the money later.'

Upstairs he has taken out everything except the front seat, making room for a double bed, fitted with an electric blanket from Canada that works off a battery 'I find I indulge myself living on the bus: champagne, caviar, that sort of thing'. Then there are two single beds running the length of the bus, and a water tank over the stairs at the back.

'Plenty of room though. We had a dance up here one night, after a wedding. I was downstairs and you could hear them all going thump, thump, thump on the ceiling.' Under more normal conditions, though, his privacy seems to be complete.

'Depends where you park of course: I mean you can't park opposite people's bedrooms. But somewhere a bit secluded you're fine. People seem to look at the driver's seat first, and if there's no one in it they assume the bus is empty. I've woken up several times in the middle of the night and seen the flashing blue light reflected on the ceiling, then you hear the police talking about what to do and then they get in their Land-Rover again and drive off. They can't very well put a ladder up and stick a parking ticket on the upstairs window.

'No, parking's not the problem. It's the breakdowns really. But I have a vast charging plant down here under the dining room table.' With the cloth over it you would not even notice the generator was there. A gas fire is burning cheerfully beside it – 'I'm not sure what happens if it blows out when we're going along, but I've an idea what *might* happen' – supplied by the same Calor Gas cylinder that supplies the cooker and the fridge. There are bus seats to sit on – 'I wanted it to go on looking like a bus' – and behind the driver's seat, underneath the electric clock, Tony's bike is stowed away. It is painted blue to match the bus and has the same number-plate.

'We had a burglar one night. Got in through the driver's cab and then got tangled up in the bike. He was literally trapped. I came downstairs and found him. We were parked over on Putney Embankment and I told him I'd got the whole rowing team upstairs and they were all going to come down and thump him. He was off pretty fast after that.'

Tony prefers to live, when he is on the bus, in what he calls the London villages. 'Putney, Hampstead, ideally somewhere on a bus route, because they cut the trees the right shape. Then I like to get the bike out, do my shopping, and come home. I mean you're paying rates in the form of taxes. I had a letter delivered once. I woke up and heard the postman knocking at the little door at the back. It was addressed to The Blue Bus, Putney Embankment.

'Mind you, I can't imagine this happening in Moscow or Spain or New York. That's what I like about the English really: they leave you alone.'

Douglas when I visited him was waiting outside the front door of his secluded vicarage, working on a 1945 Ferguson tractor he had just bought, with old tins on the vertical exhaust pipes to keep the rain out. He asked a passer-by to swing the starting handle, the engine turned over, and there was a massive bang, followed by two sharp cracks as the tins were blown sky-high and landed in a distant part of the garden. Douglas chuckled, wiped his hands on a bit of rag, and led us into the house to play one of his twenty accordions in the music room. Sitting among his serpents, souzaphones, euphoniums, tubas, trumpets and balalaikas, he opened the accordion and sniffed. 'Hello, smells as though someone's been sick over it. They have too!'

His collection of old cars blocks the wide gravel drive like a traffic jam. His 'wardrobe' is a largish room upstairs full of uniforms and riding boots, jackboots and ordinary boots, all of which he puts on from time to time when the mood takes him to drive round in his cars and motorbikes. Above that there is an attic full of old-fashioned gramophones, rusty skates, broken tickertape machines and a giant camera that once belonged to Baron. On the walls are his own primitive paintings, some of a giant orange bumble-bee hovering in a blue sky over a little village, and some of hook-nosed Russian monks drinking tea from samovars. He and his young American wife were thinking of buying a horse and cart to drive down to the village in.

Douglas talks quite happily about his days in the West End. 'I was sorry for the poor fellow who played the 'cello. It was his own 'cello, you see, and one night Tony ran it over with his penny farthing. Completely smashed. Just had this wreckage hanging from the strings, poor chap. The management bought him another one. Very decent of them.' He says he'd like to do another show, possibly a version of Beau Geste, or possibly something about pirates, and write some more music for it. But the life of a Russian landlord obviously suits him very well, and when we left he and his wife were going back to practise a tuba duet for a local music competition.

Bruce Lacey lives in a warehouse flat in Stepney, always working on some new project for a festival or an exhibition. His own collection of old wireless sets, German helmets, dummies and ornaments, some of which he is hiding from the Alberts for fear they will take them on stage and break them, are neatly stacked on metal racks in a side-room as they would have been when he was working as property master for Michael Bentine's television programmes. 'My problem with the Alberts is trying to bring them into the twentieth century. For years I was conscious of walking into the future backwards, looking into the past. Now I've turned round and faced the future. Tony will come, but Douglas won't budge. We did the *Three Musketeers* at the Royal Court, and now he wants to do pirates. Which is virtually going back even further, out of the seventeenth century, into the sixteenth.'

Wherever they are, it would be nice to hear from them again.

Edna's Better Half

Watching the monster, Edna Everage, prance across the stage in bare legs and a tennis skirt, then stop, with racket raised and tongue lasciviously extended, about to pounce on some dear old lady in the first three rows of the stalls for a public heart-to-heart about their shared experience of the menopause, you can't help wondering about the man behind the woman. Who is Barry Humphries, Edna's creator, body and brains? Where did he find what Dr Swift called the savage indignation, the rage that drives her?

In the introduction to the limp edition of her autobiography, collected cookery and beauty hints, *Dame Edna's Coffee Table Book*, the hideous Edna recalls the first time she met her maker. It was after a Passion play and pageant at Holy Trinity, Moonee Ponds. She was on her way to wash her hair in the font after playing Mary Magdalene, in the scene where she anoints the feet of Our Lord with spikenard; in this case a mixture of Valderma and Sloane's Liniment.

'I found a rather round-shouldered young man, with lank, rather grimy hair. In those far-off days Barry, who was always ahead of his time, wore his hair very long, like a modern bank clerk. He wanted me to help him in some of his stage shows. It seemed he required a talented and mature actress to "fill in" while he was off-stage changing into his strange characters. Poor boy, even in those days he considered himself a cut above everyone else, and he never stopped sneering at the lovely homes of we suburban folk. A lot of his skits were clever in a way, I suppose, but the audiences yawned and shuffled through most of them, and it soon became obvious that it was Yours Truly that they had really come to see. When I was made a Dame for my services to Australian Culture by the former Prime Minister, Gough Whitlam, I am sure poor Barry must have been terribly bitter and jealous underneath.'

Barry himself would, I think, admit that there is a grain of irritating truth in that, as there is at the core of all Dame Edna's verbal pearls. Edna, persecutor of her husband Norm the Prostate Sufferer, terrible strangler of parrots for her parrot pie, eyes flashing behind diamanté specs, dentures clenched and dazzling, has done more than simply overshadow Barry's other dramatic caricatures. Sandy Stone, the ancient, decaying memorialist of the days at the tennis club before the war, has now finally died and talks from the Beyond. Les Patterson, the ponderous, belching philistine entrusted with disseminating Australian Culture at the Court of St James, has emerged with a knighthood. Barry McKenzie, virtuoso of the Technicolor yawn, has now made two films. The figure she has threatened to engulf entirely is Barry Humphries himself.

In many ways he is his own most extreme creation, and one likely to loom fearsome in the literary memoirs of his day, as much as in the reminiscences of actors. I was going to describe him as an ex-alcoholic, but his new wife – he has two daughters by his first marriage – said he might prefer me not to use that phrase. Indeed she proved to be right. Barry said he'd rather I put 'ex piss-artist and relentless womaniser'.

But he is also an aesthete, a dandy, a collector of rare first editions, an instigator of gargantuan practical jokes, a painter and art historian: the survivor of a wildly bohemian past when he was once hungry enough for public recognition to hiss in the ear of a taxi-driver he was paying off in the presence of others beginning to make their names in television: 'Five shillings? Ten bob if you say "Thank you, Barry".'

'I think there was a great deal of frustration behind that' – we were talking of the time in 1966 when we both worked on a rather unsatisfactory television 'satire' programme called *The Late Show* – 'I knew there were some things that I was really very good at, and I had no opportunity to show them. I thought "Is it because I went to the wrong university or what?" I was really very sorry for myself, and puzzled.'

The frustration, reaching the pitch at times of an almost insane rage, seems to have been the prime force in bringing into being in the antiseptic air of suburban Melbourne the reincarnation of a turn-of-the-century aesthete, a lover of encrusted syntax and the smouldering sanctuary lamps of decadence.

Even with a smudge of Edna's mascara on his lower lid from the Dame's last press conference, Barry Humphries is solidly, unambiguously masculine. A deep voice, a mild Australian presence in the vowels, the consonants clipped and sounded, the sibilants hissing like a chisel chipping into stone. He chooses his words for assonance and internal rhymes, even in conversation, with the ironic precision of a man selecting the text for his own epitaph. There are echoes of Sandy's incoherent drawl when he remembers Old Australia, and more than a suggestion of Edna when he quotes his mother, baffled by the genetic mystery of his artistic origins: ' "*Where* did you come from, Barry? We never knew *where* you came from!" That was a favourite phrase of my mother's. And "You're making your father *sick* with worry".'

Barry's father was a successful builder in a suburb of Melbourne, his grandfather a Lancashireman who died only recently, still with a strong Lancashire accent. 'My mother's uncles were amateur painters. But they were skeletons in the cupboard, not referred to much, and given to habits, I have since learned, of *gross* intemperance, which for a time in my own life I emulated as strenuously as possible. But certainly nobody in the family seemed to *read*.'

Nor was there any direct encouragement to do so at school, at Melbourne Grammar. 'I think you'll be able to understand the atmosphere when I tell you that the Art Master was the Football Coach. It was wartime, of course, and all the younger masters were away fighting the Japs and getting malaria. They used to come back sometimes, looking very thin and very yellow, on their way to the fever hospital. So we were taught by old men who had retired in the thirties. There was one of them who had actually *met* Edmund Blunden. I was very impressed by that.' He was impressed because he had already discovered Blunden himself, as he had discovered Sassoon, and come to admire what he calls their 'dandiacal rage'. Barry Humphries's own dandiacal rage seems to have been fired by the English public school philistinism of life at Melbourne Grammar. He was mocked for his incompetence at games as Granny Humphries, and took refuge with what he describes as 'other frailer boys' in the Debating Society and the Art Society. He also founded the Melbourne Grammar School Dada Group. Their first exhibition included a pair of boots filled with custard, entitled *Pus in Boots*, a bathful of Russian salad with a single volume of poetry half submerged – *I was reading this book in the bath when I felt sick* – and an item gleaned from a sheep's carcass at the butcher's, called *Eye and Spoon Race*. The Headmaster closed it, had him into his study, and asked 'whether I didn't think I might be becoming a bit of a pansy'. Looking back at that, and at Australian culture in general, he talks about it now as 'the circumscribed life'.

But the spark of anger seems to have been struck, at least in terms of Edna's white-hot flame, a good deal earlier. 'If England is the Motherland and Germany is the Fatherland, Australia is certainly the Auntieland. Everyone seems to be dominated by their aunts. I had a lot of aunts, all very nice, but they were there, all the time. So I was pretty good at giving an impersonation, certainly, of a kind of synthesis of these women. And also of their obsession with domestic detail, seeing the whole world, really, through the Venetian blind of the kitchen window: seeing everything in terms of household arrangements, cleanliness, all that stuff. These people who managed to live comfortably and happily in such a very narrow world' – a maniac intensity comes into his voice – 'that they could get by without ever having read the Muirs' translations of Kafka, that they could be perfectly happy and well-entertained without dipping into *Cardinal Pirelli*.'

So the caricatures of these under-privileged unfortunates were launched on the world: Edna was born in a bus as the archetypal Mayoress of a small Australian town when he was touring as an actor in Beckett, Shakespeare and Ionesco with a Melbourne University company, Sandy Stone was distributed on gramophone records in the mid-fifties, to be taken up and praised by John Betjeman, a close friend ever since, and Barry McKenzie, brought into existence at the suggestion of Peter Cook in collaboration with the New Zealand cartoonist Nick Garland, when Barry was in London playing the undertaker in the original production of *Oliver!*, understudying Fagin, as he did later in New York. Their style of presentation owes something to the middle-brow theatrical tradition of Ian Hay and amateur dramatics he knew as a child, English radio comics like Tommy Trinder and Arthur Askey, and a great deal to the blacker dramatists in whose work he appeared at the University, particularly Beckett.

'In those kind of lonely, desolate figures in Beckett's work I saw echoes of Australia. It seemed to me that Australia was really a sort of Gothic place. There it was, with lots of sunshine, and everyone saying what a healthy, no-nonsense kind of civilisation it was. But it seemed to need an Ibsen, or a Strindberg, really, because there was so much real madness about. And so isolated. People kept saying "Why do you go to Europe all the time, why don't you go to South-east Asia?" I say "I was born there." In Melbourne, a strange British colony, miraculously set down in South-east Asia. As Betjeman calls it, Cheltenham in the jungle. Except that Melbourne isn't in the jungle, and it's more like Romford.'

But the dominant influence in Edna, in Sandy, or in any of the gallery of great cabaret grotesques, is the glittering syntax of the Exquisite tradition in English literature, the fruit of a lifetime of browsing in second-hand bookshops, a habit that began at Melbourne when he was still at school.

'The Debating Society and the Art Society used to meet in the evening, and, of course, it was a day school, so there was an interval, and going into bookshops in the town was a good way of filling in the time. Mrs Bird's, in particular; there used to be a Catholic priest sitting there, drinking sherry, and she'd find me books, and call me "Mr Humphries", not "Humphries"' – the philistine boom of Sir Les Patterson comes into his voice – 'like they did at school. "I think I have something that might interest you, Mr Humphries . . ."

'I was drawn to the fact that they were *old* books. For example, there was a big thing, particularly in the war, about textbooks. "Which boys are having second-hand

34

books and which are having new books?" It was a sign of who had money and who didn't, who would have to have some other boy's *Latin for Today*. And my parents always insisted that I had new books. And yet here were shops that *sold* other people's books, books that other people had *owned*. Now you can't imagine how odd that is in a country as clean as Australia. Barry McKenzie' – he follows his usual practice of referring to the character as if he were an independent person – 'once said, "Australia doesn't smell of anything." But here was a dusty shop, where things were, in fact, more expensive the dirtier they were, the older they were; the more people had owned them the dearer they seemed to be. Ten shillings I paid once for *The Poems of Lord Alfred Douglas*, autographed by Douglas: that was a great find. I've always been lucky though: like that Frank Harris I found in Edinburgh.'

I remembered the occasion: a hired black limousine at a time Barry couldn't afford it, a chauffeur with white gloves to drive us from the third-rate hotel, reeking of stale beer, where we'd been installed by the BBC, to various bookshops. The shop bell jangling, an ancient antiquarian bookseller appearing, full of erudite menace and aggressive gentility to ask our business, and Barry stopping him dead with booming theatrical confidence: 'Got any Lafcadio Hearn at all?'

Lafcadio Hearn has every possible advantage for Barry: he is suitably obscure and esoteric, the author of two rare books, *Two Years in the French West Indies*, and *Glimpses* – a word Barry always relishes – *Into Unfamiliar Japan*, in his favourite manner of late nineteenth-century decadence. 'Lafcadio Hearn, oddly enough, I found out, applied in the eighteen-eighties, the *late* eighteen-eighties, for the job of Professor of English at Sydney University, and was turned down. Think of it, if Lafcadio Hearn had been in the Chair of English at Sydney University then – an *aesthete*! – the whole of Australian academic life might have taken on a different character. He went instead to Tokyo, and so these Japanese books came out, an odd sort of mixture of Walter Pater and the Japs.'

The trick, which Barry himself has only recently come to recognise, lies in combining the outrage and energy of the cabaret with the precise, painstaking selection of images and words he has learned from literature of a particular kind. 'I used to think "Isn't it funny? I'm interested in these things, the books and so forth, and this is what I do." Now a few friends have pointed it out, and it does suddenly seem that they do coalesce, that there is a kind of consistency. John Betjeman reminded me, for instance, of the links between Sandy Stone and Mr Pooter, also invented by two people with their roots in music hall, and other writers of elaborate monologues. There is quite a tradition: George Robey, Browning and so on.'

Browning lovers may be appalled, but behind the irony, the gag, Barry Humphries is only defending the stage: the link between 'literature' and the words, sometimes never appearing in print, that are spoken in cabaret or in the music hall. 'Talking about Edna, for instance, people often say "Oh, you make it all up", but they don't realise how densely scripted it all is, and tested in the presence of an audience. A word out of place can mean the difference between getting the laugh and not getting the laugh at all.'

'I suppose there *is* a tradition in style: William Beckford, Firbank, through to people like the Sitwells and Harold Acton. I've found I share with John Betjeman and quite a lot of other people a great interest in the writing at the end of the nineteenth century: things that influenced people like Joyce and Eliot especially. A highly *artificial* style but with a very strong emotional expression. Gertrude Stein, when she was actually writing about real people and how they felt.'

I mentioned a line I particularly like, when Edna describes from the stage an unseen figure at the back of the stalls with a box of chocolates 'linked to her lower lip by a *trapeze* of dribble'. Barry Humphries, the thoughtful man of letters, in a grey pinstripe suit, a short hair-cut and well-polished hand-made shoes, considers Edna, a character he seems at times heartily to dislike, whose popularity amazes him, and who appears at times literally to have her own independent existence. 'Well, it's an aside, really, isn't it? I mean, no Melbourne housewife, glimpsing a voracious eater of chocolates in the stalls, would ever conjure up such an image. But once the character's sailing along, it's possible for the actor impersonating the character, if only for a split second, to step out of Edna, use the expression, and then quickly go back in again: so the audience say "Oh, after all, quite a wordsmith, old Edna, when she wants to be." '

Cleese

John Cleese sits hunched in a corner of the sofa, hands pushed down into his trouser pockets, shoulders up to his ears, legs crossed, moustache stretched in concentration, eyes looking vertically up at the ceiling as he thinks for a slow count of twelve about the very first occasion he can remember showing off as a child.

'It's funny, you suddenly want to get it right, actually to see if you *have* got a first memory. I think I realised that I could make them laugh, not by doing outrageously naughty things like John Darby or Robin Slaney who used to have matchstick guns and water-pistols and fire them into the back of your neck. Darby used to fire a water-pistol *in class*' – there is real awe in his voice, even now – 'and he was much admired for his sang-froid because he fired once and hit the ceiling, actually made the ceiling damp, and Darby – he was only nine or ten – managed to convince the master that it must have been raining.

'I didn't have nerve like that, but I could make quite funny remarks. Sanger-Davis had a system of giving us black S's – a black S if we were naughty cancelled out a red S for satisfactory work – and I remember, before he came into form one day, doing a forecast of what the lesson was going to be like in terms of clouds of black S's appearing from the south-east. A sort of weather forecast. But nothing that would have involved wrath from the masters. I couldn't face that. I was very much a goody-goody, so all the defiance was very muted and surreptitious. I got a history report from another man called Whitmarsh who couldn't pronounce his r's and had to spend entire terms talking about the Woyal Pwewogotive, and he wrote: "he indulges in subversive activities at the back of the room", which was absolutely right. It was always subversive, it was always small. And I've discovered that this is my nature, unfortunately. I *am* subversive, that's why I can't get involved in any institution.

'I remember my father asking a friend of mine when I was at my prep school in Weston-super-Mare, "Why does John get bullied so much?" and he said, "Well, Mr Cleese, he's so meek." I remember the fellow still: his name was Mills and he played rugger eventually for Cambridge. I think I was meek, and prominent in a physical sense, because when you're my size you can't fade into the background. I was also a loner; not by choice, just a bad mixer; an only child, not very good at looking after myself, and I'm sure in Mr Sanger-Davis's class at about the age of ten I discovered that the way to popularity was to make them laugh.'

Surprisingly for the chin-jutting wizard of the walks, the ruthless lunatic of a revolutionary leader in *Life of Brian* or the hysterically knotted proprietor of Fawlty Towers, John Cleese is still remarkably meek. The first time I met him, we were both singing in a greenwood chorus devised by Peter Cook and Dudley Moore in *Not Only But Also*. As we sat in the extras' dressing-room waiting for our Robin Hood costumes to be brought through, I formed the impression of a careful, thoughtful, rather nervous man. In a word, meek.

This time, with two glorious series of *Fawlty Towers* behind him, the whole remarkable saga of *Monty Python*, and the takings on *Life of Brian* flickering towards the twenty million dollar mark, I half expected – Basil Fawlty's mannerisms apart – something of the hysterical mood that marks those in the grip of international success: a tendency to overdo the modesty, a slightly desperate desire to put old friends and acquaintances at their ease, the general jumpiness of people who have spent too much time under the hot lights and the flashbulbs.

Not a hint of it: John Cleese is exactly the same as he always was, but more so. Meek, but on a massive scale, as if he had expanded naturally into the Big Time.

He's still a wonderful listener; he still has a huge shout of a laugh, he's still very careful choosing his words, still rather nervous, but all the time within the context of a new, solid confidence. The knees still twiddle and he crosses and recrosses his legs, the eyebrows flicker, he leaps suddenly

39

to his feet to illustrate some point of acting – all the nervous mannerisms are there – but he seems to enjoy them, like a man going through some pleasurable ritual, shaving in the morning or teeing up a golf ball.

He blames the meekness largely on class. 'I do think the middle class are so funny and apologetic: certainly the lower middle, which is the bit I know. All my friends are middle to lower middle. They're on the whole very kind people, that is to say, they're very afraid of causing pain, almost to the point of being over-protective. If someone bumps into us in a queue the most we ever do is say something feeble like "Funny people in here today" to no one in particular and look away. And really that's what Basil Fawlty is about.

'What I discovered I had in common with Connie Booth' – his wife, with whom he wrote *Fawlty Towers* but from whom he is now divorced – 'to begin with was that we both had great difficulty in expressing our anger. Both of us used to fall about when we were in a cinema or a theatre at people who were unable to let their anger out, but who were quite clearly feeling murderous inside, just having to smile and maintain the social niceties on the surface. And that's the thing about Basil: he *can't* let his anger out.'

He re-knots his legs and leans forward with a strange intensity. 'You see, people don't understand Basil. They think he calls people stupid gits. He *never* calls anyone a stupid git. All his insults are indirect because he doesn't have the gall to stand in front of someone and confront them. Unless, of course' – he throws in almost as a footnote – 'he is very occasionally driven to such a pitch that he has to. But all his insults are oblique. They're all little digs he can pretend he didn't make if the guests actually corner him, because he's not a courageous man.'

Whether or not Fawlty or John Cleese himself find it difficult to express their anger, I detected a real rumble of rage when I made the mistake of asking whether the two were related; whether Basil Fawlty was a kind of therapy for John Cleese. My reason for asking was that he and Connie Booth spent three and a half years going to a psychiatrist, trying, as he puts it, to 'sort out their thing'. I expected enthusiasm about the importance of finding the psychological truth in comedy, the need to get it out of your system and so on and so forth. I was wrong. He believes in the slow process of 'looking at' some disagreeable aspect of one's nature until one can accept it, forgive it, that there may then be the possibility of change. But he definitely doesn't believe in writing or acting as therapy and doesn't like the idea of being identified with Basil Fawlty. 'I have to admit that I am surprised by the question. A lot of journalists say, "Is there much of Basil Fawlty in you?" and I am annoyed by the *obviousness* of it. And I often throw it back at them and ask if they were interviewing Laurence Olivier and he was playing Othello, would they say, "Tell us, Lord Olivier, is there a lot of the blackamoor in you?"'

Journalists in general, despite or maybe because of an early attempt after Cambridge to make a career with *Newsweek* that failed after six months, are not among John Cleese's favourite people. 'They have these dreadful rags to fill up. Every day these journalists have a sheet of paper with nothing on to fill up. That's what journalism is: it's filling up empty paper. I suppose I talk to you differently because of our background and interests and so on. The truth is, yes. There is quite a bit of me about Basil. When the phones are ringing, and I have too much to do, and too many deadlines and I'm feeling the tension, the physical tension, there are moments when I could smash them, but I don't. And that, as I say, is what Basil is about: not letting it out.'

The phrase about himself he likes best, one applied originally to T. E. Lawrence, is that he has 'walked backwards into the spotlight'. He was never in the school play at Clifton because their major production was in the summer when he was playing cricket, and he remembers them being cast from 'bookworms'. 'There was a House Play. I think I can honestly say I didn't manifest any ability at all. We did *Seagulls over Sorrento*, in which I played a character I called Lofty. I was in a panic because I had to peel potatoes on stage and I took an entire scene to peel *one*. And I did a thing in which I got a lot of laughs, *Faust*. I was playing Lucifer. I can still remember coming through the curtains in black tights – I mean, I'm skinny now, barring the paunch, but when I was sixteen or seventeen I was the height I am now and about ten stone. I don't suppose I had a plateful of meat on me – and I remember bursting through the curtains and saying, "I am Lucifer". The audience was really meant to shrink back in horror, and I got a roar of laughter.'

There was a production of *Tartuffe* later when he thinks he may have done 'one or two things naturally' without knowing what he was up to. But nothing amounting to a stagestruck childhood.

'I had played Malvolio at my prep school. I didn't understand a word of it – still don't even now – but I probably looked right. I can still remember sitting in the Masters' Common Room, which was used as a dressing-room, having my legs cross-gartered and people putting grease-paint on my face, with a vague feeling that it was exciting, but not in an attractive way, and that it felt like show business.

'The only other time I felt it was show business was in the Cambridge Footlights Revue when we had a really appalling closing number at the end of the first half when we were dressed as cavemen. And despite the fact that it was quite the worst thing in the Revue – I mean *dreadful*: each night the curtain went down to total silence – I still felt because we were dancing and singing and doing things we had no right to be doing at all because we couldn't do them, that it was show business. And I still feel, because I do some of the things I do competently, that it's not show business. I still feel I don't belong, that I'm still dancing up and down on the touch-line while they're all in there in the big game.'

This in spite of *Cambridge Circus* touring in New Zealand, a run in New York, and a long series of shows like *The Frost Report*, *At Last the 1948 Show* before *Monty Python* ever began. 'I think it's the idea that the orthodox is the real thing. To take a man I like personally but whose acting I do not enjoy, when I see Ian McKellen act I feel "This is Shakespearian acting." I don't happen to want to watch it, but this is the Real Thing nonetheless.'

Looking back at his time at school, he is appalled at the cruelty of it: a master taken off in an ambulance with a nervous breakdown because he couldn't keep order, one boy held up to public ridicule by a master because he smelt, another told to get out of the room because whoever was teaching him didn't like his face. It was a world with which he had to come firmly to grips when he went back to teach at his prep school at the age of eighteen, before Cambridge: 'I realised it was either them or me.' The threats in the grown-up world are still there. There is, for one thing, the fear of failure: 'There's no humiliation like trying to be funny and not succeeding. An actor can go on and the thing doesn't really work but he can still come out with his pride intact. You can't do that if you're asking people to laugh. We all know that because of the efforts we make in a social circle if someone tells a rotten joke – it's a terrible feeling. But we know we can't win them all.'

There is also the threat of the Press: filling up their empty pages with what he calls 'trumpeting'. 'I must be the first person in history to refuse the front cover of the *Radio Times* for the first series of *Fawlty Towers*. Not out of any kind of modesty, because I really am utterly lacking in modesty – I know exactly what I am good at, and I'm quite pleased about it: but because it was bloody silly to trumpet it. The whole thing was to let people turn on then think, "Oh, this is quite funny". Discover it for themselves. With the second series there was such a fanfare of trumpets that you could not still, that people's expectations were raised and they said it wasn't so good as the first series.'

He is also irritated, but not much more than irritated, by critics. He can think of one notice from Alan Brien sixteen years ago about 'mugging', pulling too many faces, that he found helpful, but with a few exceptions he finds television critics very little use. 'I think Clive James is rather a good critic, for instance, but he actually spends two-thirds of his column doing the *Eurovision Song Contest* and *Miss Universe*, all the things that don't matter. Alan Coren used to review for *The Times*, probably still does. I went to a *Punch* lunch and Alan, who is a very pleasant fellow, apologised for not having reviewed the first series of *Fawlty Towers*, and I said, "That's fine". I wasn't really aware he hadn't, you don't remember them all, and then he said, "But the truth is I liked it, and I can't be funny about things I like." '

But the worst bullying, he admits, is self-inflicted. The

43

familiar problem of working against time and time hitting back, *Fawlty Towers* was, as a half-hour comedy show, only allotted five days' rehearsal by the BBC. 'That was for 130 pages. *Are You Being Served* was also a half-hour slot, and they work on a script of sixty-five pages. You just had to rely on all your experience, a lot of luck, and fortunately the BBC has the best video-tape editors in the world.' But that seems part of a general pattern: 'I seem to construct my life so that I'm too busy. Being busy involves work and work involves stress. I get into a spiral.'

If comedy began as a defence, a very strong character has grown up behind it. There have certainly been hard times: a year spent writing a film that was never made; almost worse, another eighteen months working on a script that was made without his cooperation. He plays the show biz game very coolly and competently, but his great strength, he believes, is that he knows it's a game. He was recently offered a job in the USA that would make him a millionaire in three years. 'In the end I decided that the only reason I wanted to do it was for the trip to San Francisco. Then I thought if I really want to go to San Francisco I can go there without doing the job. So I turned it down.'

The crucial experience, he thinks, was in the autumn of 1957. 'I'd had a very good summer term, I'd got my three A levels, been in the cricket team, run the library, which involved indexing things and getting cards; I'd spent hours writing up the minutes of library meetings, and I'd also run the cricket equipment for the House so successfully that we'd finished up with about four times the number of bats and pads we'd started with. I went back to Clifton at the beginning of the next term confident that I would finally, after waiting two terms longer than I expected even then, be made a House Prefect, and I found that I *hadn't* been. That there was another boy who had got two A levels, and *hadn't* done anything for the House, and *hadn't* been in the cricket team, and he had been made a Prefect instead.

'I still really don't know why: I think, even in my adolescent way, I was quite a strong personality. I mean, very weak with it' – another footnote tossed in – 'but I had facets that were strong, because I had the ability to make

44

people laugh, and you know that gives you a certain strength. And the Housemaster was a very weak man, and I think that was what it was about, but I still feel just a tickle of anger about it even now, because it was very important. But it was at that point I knew. I knew this was absurd. It's a game. It doesn't matter. It's about the only thing on which I agree with Malcolm Muggeridge.'

As a cricketer, the metaphor of the game, mattering terribly but not mattering at all, obviously appeals very much.

But listening to him, calm and confident, playing the game, it's impossible to resist the theory that Basil Fawlty really is the Dorian Gray portrait in the attic, the poor scapegoat bearing all the suffering and stress.

Crossing the Line

' "I want to warn you" ' – Milton Shulman, Canadian ex-lawyer and former crooner, relaxes urbanely on the sofa in his drawing room above Eaton Square, catching the dogmatic growl of his fellow-countryman, Lord Beaverbrook, when he appointed him *Evening Standard* theatre critic – ' "I want to warn you against the temptations that will be offered to you: they will be offering you women, liquor, and money!" And I thought to myself, "Well, this is the job I've been looking for all my life." '

Both Shulman and Frank Marcus, of the *Sunday Telegraph*, to whom I told the story, have discovered this to be a 'disappointing myth', but critics have traditionally been exposed to every kind of attempt to influence their judgment. Bernard Levin and Kenneth Tynan have both been physically assaulted, and Harold Hobson thinks that he has only escaped on account of being lame. 'If I weren't lame, you see,' he confesses, twinkling like an animated garden gnome, 'I don't know what would have happened.'

'The most famous person to have hit me,' Tynan remembers with hesitant modesty, 'although he missed, was Richard Burton. It was about nothing I'd written about him, oddly enough. He was appearing at the Old Vic at the time: he had played Coriolanus and Claire Bloom had played Coriolanus's wife. I had praised her enormously as Juliet and Ophelia, but I didn't think she was terribly good in *Coriolanus*. I wrote that she wasn't yet an experienced enough actress to play really small parts, and that she looked like a sea-lion waiting for Mr Burton to toss her a fish. I must say, I wouldn't write that now.

'Anyway, I went to a party soon afterwards – critics should always stay away from parties as a general rule – and Burton was singing some Welsh hymn in a corner with a group of rugger players, and he saw me across the room. He'd had a few drinks, and he came towards me, a well-built man with brawny shoulders, like Jeff Thomson, and said, "What was that you said about my friend Miss Bloom?" He was a very close friend of hers at the time, and he swung at me with his right. Thank God he had been at the party longer than I had.'

The victim's reaction is not always physical: one producer in America, Alexander Cohen, distributed to friends at Christmas specially printed rolls of lavatory paper with the face of John Simon, critic of the magazine *New York*, beaming up from every sheet.

In England, the counter-attack is generally more subtle. Lindsay Anderson is in the habit of writing private replies, after which, according to Tynan, 'You feel that all you can do is jump off the Post Office Tower in sackcloth and ashes.' And when he attacked *The Yellow Rolls-Royce* Terence Rattigan sent Tynan accounts of the box-office returns from every country in the world for weeks afterwards as proof he had been wrong.

The more conventional 'angry response', as Harold Hobson called it, came from Sir Donald Wolfit. 'I said on one occasion, and I was a great admirer of his, that his company acted down to its reputation. Two mornings later I received a letter in which he said, "My dear Hobson, if it gives you any pleasure to know that you have incurred the hatred and contempt of twenty-five honest and hard-working people, you should indeed be a happy man this morning. Yours ever, Donald Wolfit." It had a rather splendid roll to it, don't you think?

'Well, I was taken as a guest to the Garrick the next week, and the first person I saw there was Wolfit, who rushed across, folded me in his arms, and said, "Do allow me to put you up for membership of this club."'

As so often in such stories, the victim ends up grovelling before his persecutor, and the critics seem to feel this is their natural due. But, like satirists and hooligans who attack old ladies in the street, they all display a kind of pained wonderment when the victim does actually hit back.

W. A. Darlington, veteran critic of the *Daily Telegraph*, who was a post-graduate student under Quiller-Couch at Cambridge before the First World War, remembers playing cricket many years ago for Hampstead. 'I had this idealistic thing of never meeting actors, and then a fast bowler bowled a bumper at me and got me on the point of the elbow. And when I'd done dancing about, I asked the wicket-keep: "Is that chap an actor?", and he said "Why?" and I said "I thought he might be getting back at me for some dirty notice I'd written." '

But, considering the extent of their influence with the public, and the trepidation with which their words are read by writers, managements and actors, theatre critics as a whole receive remarkably little attention of any kind.

When I went to talk to a cross-section of them, some still working, some retired, I felt, as someone who earns at least a proportion of his income from the theatre, that I was crossing the same dangerous line that is crossed by those trying either to bribe or bully them. They are, for the most part, accessible and charming men, their names are in the telephone directory, but they are still potential allies or potential enemies of considerable power, and any encounter with them is essentially political.

Of all the ancient forms of government to survive under democracy, the theatre keeps most perfectly preserved the colourful and bloody lineaments of feudal private enterprise where everything depends on confidence. Both managements and actors, the robber barons and their savagely exploited villeins, need it to survive. Confidence decides the size of the Arts Council grant and the investors' cheques; confidence sustains the individual actor's timing and performance on the stage; confidence will determine how the audiences react. Sometimes, as in the world of party politics, or stocks and shares, the confidence is justified, and sometimes not. But the men who deal in this essential currency, advancing or withholding it like money-lenders handling credit, are the critics.

After a favourable notice, an actor can move mountains: if a critic has advised his audience to withdraw their trust, he may literally shrink and stumble over the text. A line that has been quoted in the paper as particularly witty will crackle through the theatre like lightning, bringing after it the expected thunder of applause; one that has been picked out as feeble hangs in the dead air for minutes afterwards.

It is tempting to begin by trying to put them on a level with the rest of us by examining what qualifications they have to do the job. But Tynan blocks this with a story about Oscar Levant, the American pianist and wit: 'For the last twenty years of his life he did little more than sit and grumble on television talk shows, and he was taken by a film director to see a sneak preview of that director's film. They went to Pasadena, or wherever it was, in a fleet of cars. The film was rapturously received, and afterwards the director said "What did you think of it, Oscar?" and Oscar said "It stinks", and the director said "Who the hell are you to say it stinks, Oscar?", and Oscar looked at him and said "Who the hell do you have to be to say it stinks?" '

The critic, judged on his credentials, is therefore simply someone literate enough to write, and able to write interestingly enough to be read: slender enough authority to occupy such a dominant position in the theatre.

As a group, critics cannot be said to exhibit any very solid *esprit de corps*. Loyalites certainly exist: Michael Billington has a great respect for Harold Hobson, to the extent of having been accused by one angry listener, when he spoke on the wireless, of 'even trying to talk like him'. Frank Marcus talks with affection of their favourite pastime during intervals of casting ideal productions of ideal plays with ideal actors. But they are still independent operators and make no effort to preserve a front of general infallibility. Milton Shulman describes Harold Hobson's discovery of emotional and creative overtones in what seem to be perfectly ordinary lines as 'baffling to every other critic'; and others cheerfully dismiss their colleagues in conversation as 'ignorant', 'mad', 'uneducated', or 'silly little men'.

One story from T. C. Worsley is typical, and has the advantage of being no longer likely to attract a writ for libel, as the hero has been dead for some years. 'I remember one night at Stratford, Ralph Richardson was giving an abominable performance in *Macbeth* – he has since agreed that it was abominable – and I was aware of the sound of snoring coming from just behind me. It was a critic called Stephen Williams. He was sitting just in front of the directors of the theatre, and I felt to some extent responsible, as a fellow critic, but there was nothing I could do. However, the moment the curtain was about to come down for the interval, he was awake and away to the bar. The same thing happened in the second half: snored away all through, and when I read the notices, he was the only one that liked it, and said it had been a most enjoyable evening.'

The only thing in which they seem to be united, whether out of modesty, guile, or blind innocence, is in their refusal to believe in their own power. They may sense, or even accept, the isolation that accompanies power: John Barber, of the *Daily Telegraph*, was the only one who said he would rather not discuss his work with me – although he happened, by coincidence, to have been my literary agent before he returned to being a critic – on the grounds, as he explained in his letter, that 'he tended now to avoid actors and theatre people', in order 'to preserve a sense of detachment'.

Harold Hobson says that he is 'very careful in his acquaintance' in the theatrical profession, and that he only knows the people whose work he does genuinely admire. Irving Wardle, of *The Times*, admits that the better you get to know people, the harder it becomes: 'When it comes to the point I just tend to louse up friendships really, and also perhaps to become more hostile about people I know than I would be if I didn't know them at all, simply because I'm so nervous of becoming rendered speechless through friendship.'

Others seem less conscious of the risk. Milton Shulman remembers going to a party at Peter Brook's, and Brook meeting him at the door, and saying, 'So nice to see you, you're one of the few critics who doesn't mind being kind to his friends.'

'I don't suggest that every writer and actor should try to get me a meal at Mimmo d'Ischia,' Shulman muses, 'but I find that if I'm friends with someone I do tend to give them the benefit of the doubt.'

Frank Marcus goes further. 'In cases where I know the actors or directors or the management I quite often suggest things. On occasions this has been followed. It was entirely on my suggestion that Julia Foster went to Nottingham to play *Lulu*, which made her name really. And in fact she is only one of several close friends I have who are in the habit of showing me scripts and asking my advice. They don't always follow it, but when they ask I do give it.'

If they underestimate their power to help in print, some of them also underestimate their power to hurt. Marcus, with his own experience in the theatre as playwright, actor and director, says that he is 'enormously aware' of it, and Wardle says he thinks he understands how many people feel. 'If you're attacked in print, it's like a slap in the face, particularly if you're an actor.' Worsley, too, recognises the temptation to wound maliciously and be praised for one's corrosive wit, and has resisted it.

W. A. Darlington remembers his own distress, as author of *Alf's Button*, when his colleagues on other papers sent along juniors, and even in one case a man from the City desk, to review it, in order to avoid hurting his feelings. 'I remember saying to Charles Morgan at the time: "I'd far rather have you saying it was balls than have a rave from someone else who wouldn't know balls if they saw them." '

But for Harold Hobson, easily 'wounded' though he confesses himself to be, a good sound beating can often be a benefit. 'One of the three things that have influenced me most in my career, if one can use these large terms, was when Penelope Gilliatt wrote, in an extraordinarily good article in *Encore*, that my style was excessively sumptuous. And this wounded me at the time. But this criticism, far from discouraging me, stimulated me. I thought: "After all, Penelope may be right." I thought about it a little more, and I thought: "By jove, she *is* right, I must do something about it.' So I tried to make my style *less* sumptuous. Not with entire success. It still goes on being sumptuous. But the same thing happens to actors and actresses. Damn braces, bless relaxes.'

But the central problem in trying to discuss the relationship between the critic and his victims lies in the critic's refusal to accept that he himself is engaged in any kind of combat, even when the victim is hurt enough to write to him.

Irving Wardle says how surprised he is that such letters, coming as they do from highly intelligent people, should not be more intelligent. 'It's not so much an attempt to say: "Look, you were wrong because of this, this and this, now don't you think you ought to point out these foolish mistakes you made?" It's just: "What right have you to come along and judge our work, anyway; you have a flabby mind, why don't you get out of the business, you repellent little creep?"

'I know they're just trying to hurt back, and in their situation I would probably do precisely the same thing. But not personally having been damaged I don't feel tempted to take the row up.'

It is this withdrawal into artistic neutrality, whatever avenues of attack he may leave open socially, that makes the critic, at least as long as he is writing regularly in a newspaper, so infuriatingly invulnerable. Using the circulation and weight of his paper, he may fill or empty theatres, enrich or bankrupt playwrights, make or break the actors, but he can still claim, in his own defence, to be one man, expressing his own personal opinion: he is simply a 'writer', a camera, an observer, leaving behind him old reviews as 'time capsules' in which the theatrical experience is preserved.

Wardle says the greatest difficulty that he finds is 'changing gear' into writing the review after the passive experience of watching the play; and Darlington believes the experience is so passive that he shifts responsibility on to the subconscious mind: when the lights come up, the conscious mind examines it for its reactions. 'One's not like an examiner, awarding marks as it is going on.' He remembers Charles Morgan, pre-war critic of *The Times*, who said he never knew what he was going to write when he was getting into his cab outside the theatre, but that if he had not got the first line by the time he reached the office it was going to be a hard review to write.

Both Darlington and Marcus quoted to me Desmond McCarthy's definition of the craft: 'I let the play roll over me, and when it has receded I examine the markings in the sand.' Pressed on the truth of this passive imagery – the camera, the sand – Darlington says simply that he does not feel a missionary spirit. John Barber thinks that some people may be guided by him, 'But this is not to say I consciously set up to "guide" them like a fugleman.' Not being familiar with this word, I looked it up in the dictionary and found that it means a 'soldier placed in front of regiment etc. while drilling, to show the motions and time'.

But if they are not prepared to accept that they dictate the movements and the time in theatre politics, and believe that they have in practice very little influence, Tynan, Wardle and Marcus at least admit that they would *like* to achieve political objectives. In Tynan's case, the critic has a duty to review 'what is not happening and what might be happening, as Shaw did', and he cites as an example his own demands in print, before the Establishment Club opened in the early sixties, for a breeding-ground for young satirists and comics.

Wardle sees his main objective as making war on the 'commercial machine', a kind of economic monster, capable, in his own words, of castrating a writer. 'It's not only a moral line, it's more the feeling that I think good work comes out of people having fun. And the pursuit of having fun, in terms of the work you do, is often not compatible with the line of the greatest profit motive. For that reason I think perhaps one looks suspiciously at a new writer who has been picked up by one of the big commercial managments like H. M. Tennent, rather than one put on by Michael Codron, say, or Oscar Lewenstein.'

Marcus, coming from a German literary background, is not afraid of being serious, and talks without embarrass-ment of 'being a guardian of standards'. 'My sole obligation, as I see it, is to the art of the theatre, not towards my readers or anybody else. I feel I must use any knowledge I possess to try and maintain or heighten standards of theatre in this country.' Specifically, he remembers going out on a limb to say that Orton's *What the Butler Saw* was a classic of its kind that would one day rank with *The Importance of Being Earnest*; and taking Ronald Bryden to Leicester on a wet Monday night to see Alan Ayckbourn's *How the Other Half Loves*, which as a result of their enthusiastic notices eventually came in to London.

Michael Billington, although he has gone out on limbs, notably in referring to Max Wall in the *Guardian* as a 'genius', and thinks that he may be to some extent responsible for the latter's return to popularity, is hesitant about admitting any attempt to impose his will. Writing for a London paper, he feels that what he says becomes simply 'part of the general stream of consciousness'. Shulman is more cynical, and feels he does little more than provide his readers with their small-talk for the interval.

Hobson's disclaimer of any conscious influence in the theatre is the most touching. He acknowledges probably more than his fair share of praise for the general acceptance of Beckett, Pinter and Marguerite Duras, but has lost any faith in what effect his words are going to have, 'because my most ecstatic praise can apparently produce devastating results.

'When I first saw *Waiting for Godot* – this was in my Christian period – I greatly complimented Paul Daneman, who was Vladimir, on the way in which he raised his hat at the end of the play and said, "Christ have mercy upon us." The boy is talking about a white beard, you see, Godot . . . white beard, and Daneman's line exalted me. I became suffused with emotion, and I went home and tried to transmit in my review how Paul Daneman had lifted up one's heart in this Christian manner. Well, ten years passed away – ten years, mark you – and from a hotel in Brussels, of all places, Paul Daneman wrote to me to say, "I should like to tell you that the effect on you of the utterance of those words was the exact opposite of what I intended them to be."'

Alfred Lunt, on one occasion, had to leave the stage, as an elderly lover in a play by Noël Coward, with the line 'There is still plenty of time.' Hobson was smitten to the heart – 'I am liable to be smitten to the heart by such things' – praised Lunt's intonation on the final word, and heard later that Lunt had never been able, after reading the review, to hit the line in the same way ever again. Peggy Ashcroft, after he had repeatedly praised her use of a phrase in Pinter's *Landscape*, conveyed a message to him to the effect that if he mentioned it once more she would cut it out of her performance.

What is left, for the examiners of impressions on the sand and the preservers of fugitive experience, is a doggedly bohemian creativity in isolation, all wild eyes and ungovernable inspiration.

In Michael Billington's picture, they are a race damned from the cradle. 'Built into certain people, for some reason, is this desire to go to theatres, and the imperative need to go home and write about what you have seen.'

Hobson develops the image more fully, conjuring up an irresponsible figure in smock and beret, ready to crush the marble to release his art. 'People do rather despise critics: they think they're humble parasites. They're not. They're creative writers. Simenon says that sometimes he is ill in his skin – *mal dans le peau* – and doesn't recover health in his skin until he has sat down and written his latest novel.

'This is what happens to me. On Thursdays I feel a mounting emotion within me which clamours for release, and on Friday morning it is released on the typewriter. So I don't think that either charity or spite enter into it. They are crowded out by an overwhelming emotional and creative instinct.'

As a part of the marble block beneath the artist's hammer, and having both winced under his erratic chisel and been breathed upon and made to gleam with unaccustomed lustre by his polishing sleeve, I found some comfort in what his fellow-critic Kenneth Tynan said when we were discussing charity.

'There are occasions now, I suppose, where charity would intervene, where there do seem more important things, like the prospect of death, than getting a certain sort of bad farce off the West End stage. One suddenly realises that even William Douglas-Home is facing the prospect of mortality just as I am, and that maybe one shouldn't send him to his grave too envenomed or wounded.'

Larry the Ham

On the only occasion I have ever met Sir Laurence Olivier – I tried to arrange an interview with him for this piece and got a note to say he had to be in America for a tour with the National Theatre Company – I remember being impressed first of all by the military glamour of his entrance as he exploded through the double doors of Sean Kenny's old office above The Establishment, scattering a fall-out of staff-officers and dogsbodies, and secondly by the way he called the Irish designer 'Shawnie' – even, I think, 'Shawnie, darling' – without having his nose smashed flat by a man who occasionally lifted cars on to the pavement with his bare hands.

He is the Archactor, decked out for ceremonies, like the Archbishop, as anyone who saw his seventieth-birthday tribute to Noël Coward – also 'Noëllie' in more informal moments – will have observed, and there is no doubt about his glamour or his stature. For over fifty years now – he was first spotted before the First World War playing Katharina in *The Taming of the Shrew* at a school hall in Margaret Street, Marylebone – he has drawn trembling moans from deep in the bellies of his audience with a mere turn of his head, he has thrashed them into empathetic hysteria as he has leapt and tumbled and fought about the stage, and he has coaxed them to one emotional orgasm after another with the brutal, tender or perverse use of his honeyed and skilful tongue.

His greatest and most original achievement, and the one generally overlooked in more sensitive assessments of his art, is to have survived as a popular idol since the thirties. There have been dissenting critics who have called his work mannered and artificial, but the greater volume of world reaction, from weeping fans in Moscow to screaming teenage ravers in New York right through the great fat smug majority of fashionable theatre-goers, has been devout worship. He has never hoarded his reputation, he has worked in films like *The Prince and the Showgirl* with Marilyn Monroe and splashed about in a massive communal bath in *Spartacus*, but the breathless mention of his name by the old lady at the box office still has the same note of girlish wonder in it that it had when he was throwing himself down the staircase every night in the death scene in *Coriolanus* in 1938.

This apparently reckless physical abandon, like that of a crutch-happy, microphone-stroking lead singer in a pop group, may well lie at the root of his massive popular acclaim as distinct from his critical success. The local newspaper reporter who saw his performance as Puck in *A Midsummer Night's Dream* at St Edward's, Oxford, described it as 'a little too robust', and Elsie Fogerty, his voice teacher, reacted to his ranting and arm-waving by saying that 'she didn't think we needed *that*', but neither piece of early advice has been taken too seriously. He has hurled himself bodily into every part he has ever had, he once broke both ankles leaping over a balustrade, he has sustained numerous other injuries over the years, and he is still threatening to 'bust a gut' on the opening night of his forthcoming Shylock under the direction of Jonathan Miller.

The other and even more solid basis of his popular appeal is the singer's liberties he takes with the English language. Apart from being as memorable in their intonation and accent as the best pop songs of their day, his settings of 'Cry God for Harry . . .' or 'Now is the winter of our discontent . . .' have the same mad extreme uninhibited commitment to the particular rave-up under way and the same voluntary suspension of critical self-control as the falsetto wailing of a modern group. He himself has said that people will be laughing at his interpretations of parts in twenty years' time, and with a piece of unrestrainedly romantic popular entertainment like his West Indian *Othello*, as extreme and camp in its fashionable way as the wildest eye-rolling of the silent film stars, he may well be right. But to create any fashion somebody has to go over the top, and he has gone over the top again and again with the courage and apparent invulnerability of a multiple VC in the trenches.

He is now a sixty-three-year-old pop star. He is about to see his life's ambition fulfilled in the building of the seven and a half million pound National Theatre on the South Bank, and perceptive observers describe him dominating the Theatre's temporary premises, supported and impelled by his wife Joan Plowright, with the sensitive pride of a stag dominating its own territory. Without his glamour and stature it might well not have been possible, but there are signs that the years and years and years of adulation have taken their toll. He is after all a public-school man, a member of the Beefsteak, Buck's and the MCC, and the descendant of a line of Huguenot administrators in Church and State, and it is not surprising that he feels himself from time to time uneasy in his role. He has covered his face with putty and dyed his hair so that people should see the character and not the actor. He has frequently complained that he has 'never stopped feeling a resentment that an actor should have to live in a goldfish bowl'. Being mobbed by fans has also caused him intense misery, and he has said in public that 'these people hover on a very thin line between love and loathing'. But one consistent means of escape or possibly of revenge recurs again and again, and that is his still unfulfilled ambition – only glimpsed by his public when he played Archie Rice in *The Entertainer* – 'to make people die laughing'. It is comforting, at a time when so many public clowns bore us to death with their desire to play Hamlet, to think that Hamlet himself still nourishes reciprocal ambitions.

Ben the Seventh

Probably the best-known fact about Ben Travers, his reputation as our oldest and greatest living writer of farce apart, is that he puts his feet over his head ten times every day. 'A doctor suggested I should start doing it about fifty years ago: helps the circulation. Taxi-driver said to me just recently, "I'd rather die than do it." I said to him, "In my case, I'm afraid *that* is the alternative."'

What is impossible to know without spending time in his company, is the near-miraculous intensity of his life at ninety-three. The front door of his basement flat in Marylebone was opened by his seven-year-old great-grand-daughter, Zoë, who has inherited his bright, blazing eyes, although they are brown in her case rather than blue, and I found him bringing to an end a production meeting about his new play, *After You with the Milk*. A small, bustling man in a plum-coloured cardigan, vigorously shaking hands and slapping backs, chuckling away and unquestionably in charge.

He then sat down and talked to me for two-and-a-half hours, barely stopping to relight his pipe, never missing a name or a date, and ranging over a period of eighty-five years, from matinees he went to with his mother – he actually saw Charlie Chaplin playing a messenger boy in *Sherlock Holmes*: 'He was three years younger than I was, and I remember thinking what a very lucky little boy he was to have a career on the stage. Of course, he wasn't heard of after that until he turned up in America' – to a passionate defence of the live theatre today, threatened by television, inflation, Government cuts and Value Added Tax.

'Take the case of a chap who wants to bring his wife and a couple of friends up to the West End: it's going to cost him the best part of a hundred quid by the time he's paid for the petrol and taken them out to dinner. How are you going to go on filling the stalls night after night with prices like that? Good God, in a properly regulated community the live theatre should be recognised for what it is: the one *outstanding*, *supreme* form of entertainment – far, far superior to anything in the cinema or on the box, as much a part of a man or a woman's existence as their meals or their religion; never *quite* as important as their religion, but next door to it. It's been so for seven thousand years. And that is the aspect of it that has been so terribly neglected by these *goofs* of both parties in Government.'

As he talks, blue eyes sparkling under his white eyebrows, hunched forward, puffing away at his pipe, all the vague, remote images of London before the First World War created by nostalgic reconstructions, even by newsreels of the period, are suddenly whipped off like dust-sheets, to reveal a living city, essentially the same as it is now.

It's partly in his blood: the family business of Joseph Travers and Co. that he joined in 1902 – 'It doesn't exist any more: taken over *long* ago' – was one of the oldest firms in the City, founded in 1666, and he himself is Ben Travers VII. 'They're funny, my family. Seven generations ago there were twins born, you see, and they called these twins Joseph and Benjamin, and since then the eldest son of each generation has been called Benjamin. It's become a bit of a bind, really. Rather silly. I shan't mind if my grandson is the last, but I'm the seventh and he's the ninth. Nobody ever distinguished themselves as Benjamin Travers until my great-grandfather, who was a great eye specialist, and he was Queen Victoria's Sergeant Surgeon when she was a young woman. The old boy only had one eye himself, oddly enough, but the family eyes have always been pretty wonky.' They are certainly not wonky now: just as I was leaving he spotted a collection of his plays he wanted to give me on a high shelf, scrambled up on a chair, and only very reluctantly popped on a pair of spectacles to write on the flyleaf. 'He was offered a baronetcy, but fortunately for me he declined.'

For Ben Travers, London and the theatre have always been closely linked: a cousin on his mother's side, General Burges, 'did very well in the First World War, got a VC', was governor of the Tower of London, and lent him twenty-four cannon-balls for Tom Walls to use for the thunderstorm in *Thark* in 1927. 'He said he was going to have the loudest thunderclap that had ever occurred in a London theatre or ever would, and I think he succeeded. He got this wooden staircase, and in those days stage-hands were two a penny. He had a couple of them rolling these things down the steps and another fielding side at the bottom gathering them up. Oh, we had great fun in the old days.' He has always believed, in writing farce, in making what he calls 'more or less genuine types of human beings'. 'The farcical side of it isn't in the knock-about slapstick, it's in presenting an ordinary, recognisable chap, the next-door neighbour, who has been plunged into some completely ludicrous situation.'

He has received many honours in recent years, including a CBE and an *Evening Standard* special drama award, but the *great* honour he talks about now is being paid him by his old school, Charterhouse, who are building a Ben Travers Theatre. 'It's strange, really, because no boy could have had a more ignominious career than I did. My mother was barely five feet tall, and I took after her: I was a sort of midget. I think I was the smallest boy that ever went to Charterhouse, and probably was very little taller when I left, and anything abnormal in a school boy, particularly in those brutal old Victorian days, marked one down. My first-form master was Leonard Huxley, father of Aldous and Julian Huxley, who was a splendid schoolmaster, but after that I fell into the hands of some of the most brutal, stupid and ignorant old masters you could possibly find. They were *prejudiced* against me, those masters. I could have been quite good at cricket if I'd been a little bigger, but as it was I only managed to get into the house side. And that again was typical of my bad luck. Being rather a feeble house we were drawn against a particularly strong one. They batted first, a chap called Branston and another boy called Payne. Branston later played for Nottingham and C. A. L. Payne afterwards opened for Middlesex. On this particular occasion Branston made 199 and Payne 214, and that was their opening partnership. But it was the same with school work. I think it was my size and personality they despised. In the end I left early, I think by mutual consent.

'You have to realise, though, that I was brought up in a strict, Victorian, very puritanical atmosphere. Even at one's prep school it was *fear*, always the *fear* of God, that was dinned into one the whole time. One hadn't even *heard* of sex: the word was absolutely taboo. But I had a very happy home life. My mother was a very religious woman, had four brothers who were parsons and a sister who was a Church of England nun. Nearly became a nun herself, but she had a great love of the theatre.' She took him to see Dan Leno in pantomime, Weedon Grossmith, co-author of *Diary of a Nobody*, playing a character very like Mr Pooter in a show called *Mr Preedy and the Countess*, and a play he remembers in particular called *One Summer's Day*, with Charles Hawtrey and Eva Moore: 'Twenty-five years later Hawtrey produced my first play, and Eva Moore as a very old lady appeared in a film I wrote.'

But when he left school his career as a dramatist was still a very long way off. 'What did you do with a hopeless case in those days? Only one answer: you sent him to the City. There again the stern old directors took a poor view of me and thought I'd better start at the bottom, so I became a sort of office boy. I hated commerce: absolutely hopeless at it. But I did have one lucky break: my father had to go out to Singapore to sack the manager there and appoint another one, and he took me with him. We went right round the world. This was in the year 1904. But it gave me a taste for travel, and I wasn't going to stick to 119 Cannon Street after that. So I went and joined the Singapore branch of the firm.'

It was there that he wrote his first show, a revue. 'A tremendous success: all about the native characters. It was called *Ramsamy the Amorous*.' The part he played himself was obviously vintage Travers: a Chinese rickshaw coolie, an oppressed and persecuted figure, like Hook, the butler in *Thark*, and conceived with a passion for realism. 'I just wore a pair of green shorts and very dirty ones at that. I kept them in the hen-run for three days.'

His mother died and he came back to London, where a journalist friend got him an introduction to John Lane. The publisher, being, in Travers' phrase, 'very careful about money', allowed him to work, with some support from his father, as an 'apprentice', a position he still occupied on the outbreak of the First World War, when he was twenty-seven. 'I did anything. Writing advertisements for the newspapers and hinting on the side that we'd like a nice little notice for one of our new books, right down to cutting out quotes and pasting them in albums. But I *loved* the atmosphere. Saw all the authors: Wells, Bennett – had *lunch* with Arnold Bennett.'

Success in the West End only came after the First War, when he was approaching forty. He spent the War with the Royal Naval Air Service, dropping torpedoes on the likes of Putz, the terrifying Prussian villain of *Rookery Nook*. 'Danger was always staring one in the face' – he crashed four times and was awarded the Air Force Cross – 'and yet the whole time *laughter* was such an important part of it all. That seemed to be missing in the Second War: of course conditions were different because of the air raids – there was always this dull, monotonous danger. But I think it was the British sense of humour that got us *through* in the First World War.'

John Lane proved even more careful about money in 1918, and Travers withdrew to Somerset with his war gratuity, married and settled down to write. His first London show was *The Dippers*, which opened at the Criterion in 1922. But it was his own stage adaptation of one of the novels, *A Cuckoo in the Nest*, that set the ball rolling for the great series of Aldwych Farces in 1925: *Rookery Nook* followed in 1926, *Thark* in 1927, and *Plunder* in 1928.

'Tom Walls and Ralph Lynn had had a smash-hit success with a play called *Tons of Money* that ran for six months at the Shaftesbury Theatre – opposite the Palace, at the top of Shaftesbury Avenue on the right, been a vacant site ever since the Blitz – and then Tom Walls or his shrewd advisers managed to get a very reasonable lease on the Aldwych Theatre, which throughout the First War had rather gone off the theatrical map, and had even been a YMCA part of the time, and they transferred *Tons of Money* there. Ran for a year or so, and was followed by another great success,

It Pays to Advertise. Then for some reason or other the bottom fell out of *It Pays to Advertise*, and George Grossmith's son, Lawrence, Weedon Grossmith's nephew, who was an agent in Australia and had already interested Gerald du Maurier in my play, sent them *A Cuckoo in the Nest*. Apparently they'd already looked at hundreds of scripts, but Tom Walls read it and said "Yes", Ralph Lynn read the first act and said "Yes".'

It was obviously an explosive partnership: Tom Walls always playing the blustering womaniser, Ralph Lynn his foil, more genteel, getting in the way, putting his foot in it. 'They came from very different backgrounds. Ralph Lynn's father had been an officer in the Indian Army who had died young and left the family on their beam-ends. He played the same stock character in every show, always wore an eyeglass, a wonderful improviser, but he'd always listen to reason. Tom Walls was altogether different. He was the most dominant figure I've ever met in the theatre and he directed every play. He was that masterful type. Masterful not only with characters like myself who give way about everything: he could *dominate* almost anybody with his personality; and his position, of course, what he could offer. Wonderful character actor. Very good at old men parts. He came from the backwoods of Coventry. Been a policeman. The streets of London in those days were crowded with prostitutes, and they got more expensive as they got further West, from Piccadilly down to Bond Street. By some shocking bit of miscasting the first job Tom Walls got as a policeman was night duty in Bond Street. He used to take the ladies and interrogate them up against the wall.' Travers wipes his eyes and chuckles with pure delight. 'His career in the police force didn't last very long.'

There then followed a period of working in films, first on the Aldwych Farces – 'Tom Walls directed them, of course: the first time he ever entered a film studio was to direct a picture' – and later original work specially written for the cinema in the thirties. He also wrote *Banana Ridge*, in which he revived the ghost of the Chinese coolie of *Ramsamy the Amorous*, and played the part himself.

'*Spotted Dick*, a new farce with Robertson Hare, had

only been running eight days when the war broke out. I hated the Second War. I was much too old to do anything active except hang about Ministries of Information.'

After the war there was a long period, from his mid-fifties until he was over eighty, when his name no longer appeared in lights in London. 'I've always been tremendously self-critical: written everything six or seven times, and I didn't want to do anything that would let my reputation down. When I was young the old boys I knew personally, like Pinero and J. M. Barrie, they couldn't stop. They'd either lost the knack or they'd gone out of fashion – I think this is almost true in the case of Shaw too – and they sort of dwindled out. I never wanted to do that.' More important, his wife died in 1951. 'Everybody in the theatre loved her; I remember Ralph Lynn sent me a telegram: "Oh that lovely woman." I'd had a very happy home, nice children and all that, and I felt there wasn't much object in going on.' For fifteen years he spent the winters abroad, travelling back to Singapore and the East. 'I teamed up with a very clever, rather difficult woman called Cynthia Simpson, an Australian, part-owner of a sheep farm out there, and she lived in London in Trevor Square. I went and lived there, with her, as a PG. But I never really got down to writing anything.' Then, like a glorious and almost infinitely prolonged happy end, more glorious and more infinitely prolonged than even the most romantic screen-writer would ever have dared to provide, his public returned. Brilliantly directed revivals, like Anthony Page's production of *A Cuckoo in the Nest* and the recent run of *Plunder* at the National Theatre. 'Which, I think, proves, without wanting to sound in any way arrogant, that there is something in the old farces after all,' and the tremendous success of a brand-new play, *The Bed Before Yesterday*, in 1975. 'That was, I think the most delightful experience I've ever had in the theatre. To stop rehearsals and have a discussion with the director, Lindsay Anderson, and Joan Plowright, the leading lady, about some little passage or line, even about a syllable or an inflection, was the most fascinating experience.'

When I left him, cracking open a can of Long Life to drink with the sandwich he has for lunch, he was talking about a new play of Alan Ayckbourn's he'd just been sent. 'I have a *terrific* admiration for Alan. I think he's absolutely the joy of the British theatre at the moment, but otherwise I don't have time to read much. I'm always *working*, you see. I'm well over ninety-three years old now, can't have much longer to live, and I want to do anything I have still in my mind to do.' He has an unshakeable faith in the survival of the spirit and if he does feel any qualms you'd never guess it from the serene chuckle. He puffs at his pipe and adds, 'Let's hope they'll be produced *post mortem*.'

The Ram of Mouton

In August 1977 the blue air of Bordeaux above the vines of Château Mouton-Rothschild trembled to the roar of helicopters coming in low overhead, about to land. As in any ultra-modern vineyard Mouton's immaculate waist-high rows of vines are familiar with the noise of helicopters: any attack by leaf-rot or caterpillars, that twenty years ago would have ruined a vintage, is countered nowadays with instant helicopter intervention, trailing chemical sprays across the even green that slopes away unbroken to the far horizon.

But on this occasion the helicopters carried military markings, and soon a cavalcade of French army cars was moving at a stately pace up the avenue of white gravel that leads from the public road, the boundary with the adjoining property of Pontet-Canet, to the white stone magnificence of the Rothschild Château. Through the leafy park, until 1933 the independent property of Mouton L'Armailhacq, through the vines, and up to the high black railings of the gate into the inner courtyard.

There the passengers got out: they were wearing laundered green uniforms and discreet, red-backed stars in their caps; an arms-buying delegation of the Chinese High Command on an official visit to what has become, in the last fifty years, one of the great centres of French prestige in a country that supplies wine to the whole world. The Chinese Generals were welcomed and led through into the courtyard, also of gravel, raked daily in the Japanese style in perfect furrows: high green trees surrounding Petit Mouton in the middle, the small late Victorian house from which the surrounding magnificence has grown: on one side the great *chai* – a pagan cathedral built in 1927 to house rank on rank of pale oak barrels: on the other the Wine Museum, containing a million pounds worth of gold and silver drinking cups and ceremonial vessels: beside it the *cuvier* with its gleaming twenty foot high copper vats. They were led on through the cool marble flagged hall of the new house, Mouton itself, that forms the third side of the courtyard, and up the curving staircase to the Long Room.

There, lit by seven semi-circular windows that look out on the unbroken sea of vines, the Communists found themselves standing in their neatly polished boots on a floor gleaming with pale blue and orange tiles, under a ceiling apparently supported by a straggling frieze of golden reeds, among weird and wonderful antiques, including a life-size carved wooden horse, and being introduced to the Proprietor, Baron Philippe himself. A gentle large-domed sage in a South American poncho, check trousers and carpet slippers, greeting them on a priceless carpet by an immense wolf-skin covered sofa before his sixteenth-century baronial fireplace.

The Chinese Generals asked a question and, on hearing the answer translated, put their heels together and bowed. They had been told something they might not have suspected from the solid Rothschild proportions, the sly twinkling eyes and the firm handshake of a man who swims 800 metres a day – that he was seventy-five.

Whether or not his encounter was a direct cause of the subsequent change in China's attitude to the West, their respect for this irredeemable Capitalist, this Merchant Prince of a living dynasty that rose in the age of Napoleon and shows no sign of allowing itself to be dethroned, had more to it than mere comic incongruity.

At first sight it was a political cartoon, Revolutionaries came to pay homage in the Drawing Room, Idealism bowing to Inexorable Economic Necessity, individual merit, the heirs of equal opportunity acknowledging inherited privilege, the old exclusive order. All that unquestionably was there, but the confrontation was less clear cut than it appeared. Philippe de Rothschild, in the feudal and feuding world of Bordeaux, is still thought of as a flashy, self-made man. Admittedly Rothschild money bought Mouton in the first place, nearly 150 years ago. His inherited Rothschild wealth bailed the Baron out several times in early, more precarious years, but Mouton remains to a very great extent his own creation: the work of a doggedly obstinate poet-publicist who devotes the same relentless perfectionism to the lettering on the labels of his bottles as he does to the rhymes and rhythm of his translations into French of Christopher Fry, English Elizabethan verse and drama.

His daughter, Philippine, who scarcely needs to earn the money, has spent all her adult life as a working actress in the theatre, first at the *Comédie Française* and then for Jean-Louis Barrault, as Philippine Pascale, and it is a belief in making your own name that she clearly inherits from her father.

Everything at Mouton is the product of present energy rather than the slowing momentum of energy expended in the past. Nothing in fact is what it must have seemed to the Chinese: the gold frieze in the Long Room is painted plaster, the inspiration of an American designer: the sixteenth-century fireplace does not belong to the house but was brought piece by piece from central France when an historic building was demolished. The Long Room itself was never meant for human beings to live in: it was until the Baron's time, seven semi-circular windows and all, the hay loft over the stables, just as the inner courtyard of perfectly raked gravel used to be a midden, with stalls for the oxen that pulled the ploughs.

Even the quarter-mile drive of white gravel was built at the end of the last war, on the insistence of the Jewish Lord of the Manor whose non-Jewish wife had nonetheless died in a concentration camp – she refused to join him in London when he escaped through Spain to join de Gaulle – by the same Germans, now prisoners of war, who had occupied Mouton when it was Headquarters of a German Flak Division.

In fifty-odd years he has scandalised the Bordeaux wine establishment, first by introducing *château* bottling, by marketing a non-château Bordeaux wine under the name of *Mouton Cadet*, by having endless passionate and public love affairs, by commissioning artists including Picasso, Braque and Andy Warhol to illustrate – blasphemy of blasphemies – his wine label, and finally having Château Mouton-Rothschild officially recognised for what he believes it should have been ever since the famous classification of Bordeaux wines in 1853, a *Premier Cru*, one of the five great red wines of the region.

The energy that achieved it is evident in every aspect of his daily life. He is awake soon after six, shimmering, as Wodehouse would have said, bare-footed into his bedroom in an exquisite fifty-guinea frail linen night-shirt that often seems to double as a day shirt later, to switch on an old electric kettle and make himself a cup of tea. He then jumps back into his stainless-steel four-poster, overexciting his golden retriever Rajah who sleeps across his feet and is harried throughout the day in English – 'Raj-Put! What is it then? Raj-Put, where is your ball, eh, where's your ball?' – until the dog has performed a series of sneezing, gruffly-barking pirouettes on the perfect linen coverlet and collapses once again to doze.

The Baron then pulls towards himself various wicker work trays containing dozens of freshly sharpened lead pencils, rubbers, paper, a series of special telephone books – the numbers written on sheets of card loosely tied with ribbon so they always open flat – seizes up the telephone and begins to create merry hell for business associates, business competitors, and anyone else silly enough to answer the telephone at that time of the morning (or it may be night), from Los Angeles to Bangkok.

Everything at Mouton is theatrical – he himself, at his father Baron Henri's instigation, built and managed the Théâtre de Pigalle as a young man – but early morning negotiations are conducted as if the bed was upstage centre in an Opera House seating 5,000. The telephone, the stainless steel uprights of the bed, the linen canopy, the whole room, all vibrate to the driving boom of the voice. '*Ecoutez!* . . .' The hand that isn't gripping the telephone jabs and gesticulates, the broad dome glows with energy, the eyebrows fly up and down, wrinkling the forehead like the bellows of an old accordion, the face darkens with rage and then is radiated with sudden sunlight. The voice grows more soothing and the shattered victim at the other end is coaxed back to consciousness and cooperation.

Those who have done business with him describe the '*Contre-Proposition*' – the first blow in the bargain, probably offering approximately half the price demanded –

70

as like being hit with a steam hammer, still delivered with all the energy that lifted the family in the space of one generation from the ghetto in Frankfurt to dominate the courts of Europe. Literary collaborators – I have been privileged to assist from time to time on translations into English – are not spared. The telephone rings long before eight: a blundering hand gropes automatically to pick it up, and I have heard myself, my eyes shut, lying to the effect that I have been awake for some hours. 'A little problem' about the rhythm of a line, and the conversation proceeds at his end at least with all the concentration, agility of mind and ability to absorb suggestions that most people are only capable of at a full-scale working conference in the dynamic middle of the day.

By 10.30 a great many little sheets of paper have been scribbled over, pencilled notes rubbed out, scribbled over again and pinned to other pieces of paper. The long suffering Mlle Némoff, a severe but philosophical spinster with spectacles, a grey bun and, thank God, a highly developed sense of humour, who has been shouted at to make the necessary telephone calls so far, now comes in to be shouted at in the flesh, mutter '*Oui, M'sieu le Baron*', collect the scribbled sheets and type them up.

As she takes them away a maid in a pink overall, one of six working in various household capacities, referred to by a frequent and irreverent guest, Joan Littlewood, as the Ballet Rose, arrives with breakfast: soft boiled eggs, marmalade, pounded up with a wooden spoon in a huge cup, and another huge cup of tea, an English taste to which he attributes his sparkling health and excellent digestion. That and the swimming. In Paris where he lives in a tiny house behind the Hôpital Cochin, in an unfashionable part of Northern Paris opposite the hospital's concrete mortuary, the swimming takes place at 12.00: at Mouton, in his own glass-walled blue-tiled indoor pool, at 7.00 in the evening: a methodical submarine, only the black goggles, solid tum and black flippers visible above the water, ploughing up and down for 20, 30, sometimes 40, lengths.

In either case, what is left of the morning is given over to receiving business callers, many of whom are still surprised to find the Baron in bed.

71

Lunch, in the little dark dining room in Paris, he eats, on the rare occasions when he is alone, continuing a life-long fascination with anything feminine, watching a kind of intellectual Woman's Hour on television called *Aujourd'hui Madame*. At Mouton lunch may be served anywhere: in the library, in the Long Room, in summer under the coloured glass porch of *Petit Mouton*. The table is invariably decorated with a few wisps of grass, a quaint tangle of twigs or a bunch of wild flowers, a concept devised by his second wife, Pauline.

It is brought to the table by Kun, a Vietnamese law student in his mid-twenties in white coat and white gloves, who under the Baron's tutelage has become the best man-servant he has ever had.

Pauline, born Pauline Fairfax Potter, a French American eccentric beauty who was, among many other things, chief designer for Hattie Carnegie, and who lives in the memory of all who knew her as one of the most elegant and intelligent women ever to come out of America, remains the presiding feminine influence at Mouton where she spent the last twenty years of her life.

It was she who encouraged Marie la Fleur, responsible for the flowers in the house, to bring in the grasses and the wild flowers, she who inspired the Museum, she who supported him through the long struggle to have Mouton officially recognised as a *Premier Cru*. She, who rather languidly would leave samples of material lying over chairs for years, waiting until the final scheme would reveal itself. The Baron, patient enough in the face of the slow rhythm of the seasons, would fret at the long delays in decorating the house. 'We'll be dead before it's finished.' 'You can die if you want to, Museau, I shall not.' Tragically, she was wrong. She died in 1974 and the Baron battles bravely on alone.

But it is her work that he sees to a great degree as he strolls in the afternoon, encouraging the troops: bullying M. Conte, the architect, about the completion of a car-park wall, planned with Pauline as a perfect circle; talking to the designer about the proportions of the illustration on next year's label; negotiating patiently with the Mayor of the local village about buying an old chicken coop that can be razed to make more space for vines. There is the daily visit to M. Raoul Blondin, grandson of the great Blondin who went over the Niagara Falls in a barrel, the grey-eyed, wise *maître de chai*, who lovingly shows visitors around the cellars by candle light, full of the mystery of the place, the poetry of the life of the wine in the bottle, surviving and changing even after 100 years. Pauline's 'Petite Hollande' for the ducks, Pauline's library – another part of the hay loft – Pauline's decision on the turn of the wall to conceal a yard full of washing so that Mouton, white and stone-faced now, the idealised, luxurious, theatrical dream of a French wine-growing farm, should float alone and unmolested among the vines.

The energy is in evidence at Mouton in the evenings too when he entertains: the Queen Mother came to stay in 1976 and appears to have been delighted by the Baron's caressing warmth: but whoever it is, a visiting photographer, an American wine expert or an old friend from the twenties in Paris, he seems the same: chuckling over the riddles on the little plates he bought just after the war for practically nothing, crooning with pleasure when – in the presence of some of the best cooking in France and wines that are announced, in their anonymous tall-necked beribboned *carafes*, like distinguished guests before they are poured – a well-rinsed slug crawls out of the salad and on to the embroidered table-cloth: 'Aha! How are you, my poor little chap? What an adventure for you!'

Energy was at its most extreme one evening in the spring this year, in Paris, on a seven-hour evening at the theatre, that he still loves as passionately as ever. A matinée of a new play at the Odéon, back home for dinner, and then out again for a late performance, starting at 10.00, of a glorious knockabout farce in Montparnasse called *Le Gros Oiseau*, featuring a six foot rabbit, a small grimy angel in a beret capable of performing conjuring tricks, and a fly-eating idiot office boy finally passed off as the illegitimate son of Adolf Hitler.

When we came out of the theatre, long after midnight, the hire car – hiring a car, according to the Present Energy philosophy, is always cheaper than owning one – was blocked into a narrow side street by a number of cars. Taking off from traffic lights with the Baron, who used to be a racing driver, is always fraught with Present Energy, insisting as he does on reaching the lights opposite before they have begun to turn to amber, and Present Energy asserted itself now.

The parked cars were all, fortunately, unlocked, brakes could be taken off but they were too heavy to move. 'Get in! Get in!' A gentle acceleration, the cars were nudged back along the pavement and a gap eventually cleared. A voluble drunk outside the café at the corner shook an admonitory finger: it was not permitted to behave in this manner. *'Oui, Oui!'* The Baron nods agreement: he knows, he knows. Roaring home, he reflects resignedly on the French character. 'That's the trouble, you see. They all believe they are the sole guardian of the law.'

But Philippe as the battering ram of Mouton alone could never have succeeded: in pioneering château bottling, as he did in the twenties, in establishing *Mouton Cadet* – originally Mouton wine in the early thirties when the vintages did not in his opinion justify the château label – as a best-selling table wine all over America; in having the famous classification of 1853 revised, in the face of dogged opposition; in marrying Pauline, or in captivating, whatever their prejudices, practically everyone that meets him. Doors, admittedly, have been closed against him: complaints have been made about his pushiness, and about his friendly habit of stroking his hostess's bottom almost before he has been introduced, but there is the charm of Energy, and there is also great Energy of charm.

I wondered, for instance, why Kun, the Vietnamese law student, should have thrown himself so whole-heartedly into becoming the best man-servant he has ever had: some time ago I noticed his traditionally impassive face pucker with irritation when his method of cutting and serving a mango at lunch was criticised by the Baron and compared adversely to the way it was done at a restaurant called *La Route Mandarine*. A few days later I got back after dinner to find Kun unusually cheerful. The Baron had driven him to the other end of Paris, taken him out to dinner, and made the head waiter demonstrate their method of cutting a mango. I think probably even the Chinese Generals would have approved.

After You, Claud

I first met Claud Cockburn at the height of the Profumo Crisis. The whole of London, and in particular the *Private Eye* office over the betting shop and the striptease club in Greek Street, was rustling with the most outrageously funny rumours about our betters, and Claud, suitably enough, had come over from Ireland on the invitation of Richard Ingrams to edit a single issue of the magazine. Re-establishing, in the best traditions of the old rebel hero returning from a long retirement to answer the call of the people, many of the old contacts he had made when he was editing *The Week* from the Café Royal and the little attic in Victoria Street during the thirties, he had uncovered various astonishing and, for the most part, authentic stories behind the Profumo Scandal itself; had stuck into the magazine for those foreign spies who did not already know it a cutting from *Who's Who* giving the name and address of the head of MI5; and was in the process of putting together, from the bar in the Coach and Horses, the real story of Harold Wolfe, a man who died in prison under somewhat mysterious circumstances and whose case the newspapers preferred at that time to ignore.

Wearing, even on a hot day in the summer, a long blue overcoat with the buttons coming off it, every pocket crammed with hastily folded and rolled up papers, a frayed cigarette always hanging from his lower lip or being flicked between his long brown nervous fingers – other cigarettes burned unnoticed in various ash-trays and saucers as the story grew more involved – the bright, rather sunken eyes behind the horn-rimmed spectacles given an expression of baffled innocence by the leaping black eyebrows above, and his deep drawling voice hesitating with wicked delayed timing on some final damaging fact or hilarious irrelevancy, he had already all the rich glow of a living myth.

The overcoat had almost certainly been through the

Spanish Civil War with him, the crumpled trilby looked as though it had been stamped on by fascist thugs in Isherwood's Berlin, there was something oriental about the rather beautiful movements of the hands as he talked, recalling his birth in Peking: it was possible in more fanciful moments to believe that one was in the presence of some incarnation of the century itself, beaten up, only alive by a miracle – he had almost died of tuberculosis in Ireland – occasionally slightly drunk, but infinitely wise and still funnier than Laurel and Hardy and the Marx Brothers put together.

What was so immediately arresting listening to Claud talk was his instinctive revaluation of all values, his absolute refusal to recognise the Emperor's new clothes. 'Go into er . . . man's office, leather-topped desk, gold cigarette lighter, expensive pictures all over the walls, knee-deep carpet, deep leather armchairs . . . now you or I would immediately say the chap's er . . . bankrupt.' Men, in his stories, might command the destinies of the world, but they still wore nothing that could conceal them from the prying eyes of Claud. The brightly coloured robes and regalia of political office or social eminence miraculously disintegrated and vanished away, leaving visible in every case the bashful nude or leering satyr.

To powerful men, accustomed to being seen in this state by locker-room chums and chaps who belong to the club, the spectacle of Claud gleefully pressing his nose against the glass of the little window round the back, and – far worse – encouraging members of the general public to do the same, must always have been distressing. Such glimpses are reserved for the rich. It was, however, Claud's lifelong belief that such glimpses should be stolen, and furthermore distributed post-haste to a grateful poor.

The fact that every politician thus undressed inevitably seems to have shaggy thighs or at least a cloven hoof, that every bishop once unfrocked is found without fail to have the actress's name tatooed in an erotic cartouche on his left buttock, would seem on the face of it likely to engender in the voyeur a certain cynicism. I even went so far, in an interview with the *Sunday Times* about *Private Eye*, to describe Claud as the most profound cynic (giving both words equal weight) that I had ever met. This remark seems to have shocked him deeply. He quotes it on the final page of his autobiography, *I Claud*, and follows it up with a strong denial, concluding with a reaffirmation of his fundamental optimism and his basic faith in the adaptability and ingenuity of man.

I must confess, after reading *I Claud* – his three previous volumes of autobiography, *In Time of Trouble*, *Crossing the Line* and *View from the West* all rolled into one with additional chapters to bring us through the *Private Eye* period and up to date – that I was wrong, or at least only partly right. Whatever profound and noble cynicism Claud might display in examining the conduct of those we have set over us, the radiant creative optimism that pulled him through fifty years of debts, disasters, wars and personal tragedies was as luminous and inspiring as a religious faith. The sense of creative playfulness under the very sledge-hammer of death is so great that the book reads now in this complete form more like an epic work of fiction, with every perfectly worked anecdote, every lunatic confrontation with Al Capone or General de Gaulle fitting into the great novel of the twentieth century as if it had been imagined and created purposely to highlight or counterpoint the major tragic historical themes.

In 1966 we began to collaborate on a political farce commissioned by John Neville for the new Nottingham Playhouse, an adaptation of *The Knights* by Aristophanes, finally called *Listen to the Knockingbird*. I soon realised that Claud was not, in any sense of the word, a collaborator. He had rented what he described a 'very commodious apartment' in Cornwall Gardens, and I turned up every morning to be entertained by a wonderful flood of anecdotes, his wife Patricia chainsmoking away in the background, a permanently comforting presence providing coffee and the occasional prompt, and went away every evening agreeing we really must get something down on paper. We did occasionally discuss the shape of the play: a collapsible set designed by one of Sean Kenny's assistants to represent Great Britain as a semi-derelict brothel run by Britannia, with two dishonest commercial travellers living in the attic. Since the Lord Chamberlain still imposed theatrical censorship in those days, they had to be called something else, but they closely resembled Harold Wilson and Sir Alec Douglas-Home.

The most interesting moment in our discussions came when we reached the 'constructive' moment at the end, where Britannia was to be rescued. Who were the heroes to be? The Working Class? That was, in fact, the solution I rather naïvely came to. Claud, on the other hand, smoked a lot of cigarettes, narrowed his eyes, coughed a bit, traced a few patterns in the air with his fingers, and said he thought it ought to be 'er . . . ordinary chaps called out in the middle of the night in their dressing-gowns to deal with something like a fire.' Meanwhile the actors were waiting for the script. Claud did complete one very good monologue for Alec Home talking about a machine for regulating the economy, but the rest I had to knock together in a scandalously short time, typing Act Two in a boarding house in Nottingham while the cast started on Act One, and the result was not by any means as good as it should have been.

Nevertheless it was typical of the effect Claud had on people that John Neville, interviewed on the radio when he left Nottingham years later, said that the best moment he could remember was sitting in the Playhouse with Claud when he came up to look at the final rehearsals.

There was also a night of farce at the theatrical lodging house. Claud had obviously stopped for a few drinks with the actors on the way home, and the landlady, Mrs Parson, gave me a very beady look when I got down to breakfast. 'A very strange man, your friend.' I asked her what she meant. 'Arrived at the front door, I showed him to his room, asked him whether there was anything he wanted, a cup of hot milk or Bournvita, and he said no, all he'd like was something to read, it would help him to go to sleep. So I went and fetched him a copy of *Argosy* and when I came back the door was still open, and there he was, fast asleep, face downwards on the bed, with all his clothes off.'

He had, I discovered later, subsequently woken up somewhat disorientated, and while looking for the lavatory had trodden on Mrs Parson's Siamese cat and thrown open the door of Alastair Sim's bedroom, who had sat bolt upright in bed saying 'Ah, good morning Mrs Parson,' thinking it was breakfast time. I saw Mrs Parson years later when she had read Claud's work. 'Think of it,' she said, 'entertaining angels unawares!'

Claud's lone endeavour at the typewriter was awe-inspiring. What he called 'er – tap tap.' He began early in the morning – 'Ideally at seven. God gets up at half past nine and starts buggering you about, so that gives you two and a half hours' – either in the little downstairs room at Youghal, among a litter of browning papers, or on any flat surface he could clear in the flat in London. He wrote his column for the *Irish Times* the week he died, and scribbled a note to *Private Eye* almost immediately after he had a stroke some months earlier – 'teaching myself to type with the other hand'.

Not that he didn't occasionally dodge a deadline. The first editor of the *Sunday Telegraph* received such graphic descriptions on the telephone from Claud in Ireland of the storms and tornadoes that had prevented his copy getting through that he was heard gravely dissuading other members of the staff from taking holidays there; and the creative input that went into the excuses was certainly as great as that required to write a piece. Ingrams and I were waiting for his column one afternoon when he rang to say he was having trouble finding a taxi. Ingrams urged him to get a move on. An hour or so later the telephone rang again. 'Er . . . bit of bad luck. Running for a taxi, knocked down by a car. Er . . . fortunately very charming Indian doctor on hand, brought me back here, plying me with drink, seems churlish to refuse, so maybe er . . . a bit late.' Again Ingrams expressed mild impatience. The third call came towards the end of the afternoon. 'Er . . . extra-ordinary piece of luck, Indian doctor friend has an invitation for tea at Downing Street, asked me to go along er . . . good copy . . .' At this point Ingrams, uncharacteristically, said 'Shit.' 'With you in ten minutes.'

There were endless stories about his drinking. He was staying with me once, and I went out in the morning leaving a fairly well-stocked drinks cupboard. When I got back in the evening, Claud said there had been a telephone call for me. 'Friend of yours, Michael Hill. Wanted to ask him round for a drink, but er . . . no drink!' Similarly with money. He surprised Peter Cook on one occasion with a sudden request for a loan and Peter asked him how much he wanted. Two hundred? 'Four.' Also, despite Patricia's exemplary cooking, housekeeping and perfectly tended garden, there was chaos at the house in Ireland, with the daft maid pulling the dining room curtains and bringing down not only the pelmet but also most of the brickwork over the window, and Sonny the odd-job man, who worked there 'for the intellectual conversation', appearing at the front door, his normally rather ferocious appearance enhanced by blood-soaked hands and forearms from skinning a rabbit, sending an American research student running away down the drive in terror.

Claud was in fact an idealist, and a very disillusioned idealist. 'If God lived on earth, people would break his windows.' His best stories were wrested from setbacks that would have left lesser men depressed and silent. He was once summoned to see his son Alexander's housemaster at Gordonstoun, and arrived suitably dressed but without his socks. Claud did not apologise or invent any simple excuse. 'Found I was sharing a sleeper on the train with a Sikh. Er suggested a bit of dinner. No go. "We Sikhs do not eat this food, but by God we drink." Few drinks, climbed into the upper bunk, dozed off. Woke up, looked over the side, Johnny Sikh taking his turban off. Sees me watching him in the mirror. Terrible thing. Seeing a Sikh without his turban, certain death. Lay there all night, trembling, waiting for him to stab me in the back. Woke at dawn, still hadn't stabbed me. Bugger had stolen my socks and thrown them out the window.'

When I saw him for the last time, in London this summer, he looked terribly old and terribly feeble. I had to lean down to hear what he was saying. Same voice, same timing – 'Stroke, heart attack, cancer of the throat, double cataract all in one year: if you were writing a book people might say er . . . you were overdoing it' – and then the same laugh. I think it was because of, rather than in spite of, his faults that Claud was one of the best men I've ever met. He produced a remarkable family and a lifetime's worth of seriously funny work: if he didn't hold facts in too high a regard when retelling stories he certainly respected their fundamental truths. The word integrity is much misused, but if it means life being all of a piece, Claud had it.

Ingrams of the *Eye*

In a sane world, Malcolm Muggeridge once said, Richard Ingrams would be Editor of *The Times*. Under the present arrangement he is captain of his village cricket team in Berkshire, father of two, a not ungifted 'cellist, pianist and water-colourist, fourth of five sons who were brought up alternately Catholic and Protestant in order of seniority, sufficiently eccentric to go about in tweed jackets made fifty years ago with his shirt hanging out, and the Editor of *Private Eye*.

The first time I saw Ingrams, although we did not in fact meet until three years later at Oxford, was in 1957 in a small wooden chapel at Inchon on the west coast of Korea where he was playing the harmonium at Matins. There was, in fact, a Captain in the Educational Corps who occasionally visited our own barbed-wire enclosed barracks near the 38th Parallel, who said several times that I should meet his immensely amusing Old Salopian Sergeant, but I did not at the time realise he was talking about the incongruous, baboon-like figure at the harmonium, eyebrows raised and hands moving straight-fingered over the keys with apparent disregard for any little musical infelicities more sensitive spirits might deem to detract from the overall impression.

I think it is this businesslike simplicity of approach to whatever he is doing that is his most striking quality. Almost everyone I have ever met who writes at all has a tendency at times to tear the paper out of their typewriter and start again; but even at Oxford I remember Ingrams covering sheet after sheet with his large round hand-writing, usually in Biro, occasionally drawing a line through two or three words, but otherwise ploughing straight through to the end.

This may be an inherited gift – in addition to coming from a securely patrician background as the son of a banker, he is the great-nephew of Maurice Baring – but it does seem fundamental to everything he does. Certainly, without it he would not have been able to get *Private Eye* out fortnight after fortnight, through disastrous libel actions, newspaper strikes and, worst of all, in the summer, week after week of political torpor and general tedium. It is also perhaps typical that he never really intended to edit *Private Eye* in the first place.

Organically, *Private Eye* is simply a continuation of *The Salopian*, the Shrewsbury school magazine. Ingrams wrote for it with William Rushton, Paul Foot and Christopher Booker. Booker then went to Cambridge, but Ingrams and Foot continued together at Oxford with a paper called *Parson's Pleasure*, which distinguished itself by attracting a writ for libel – typically enough for accusing a member of a famous newspaper family of being a homosexual – and then *Mesopotamia*, for which William Rushton, who was working in London, used to come up, trailing a broken umbrella and wearing a pork-pie hat, to do the drawings. But when they came down from university it was Booker and Rushton, from Rushton's bedroom in Scarsdale Villas, who produced the first duplicated, yellow-paper edition of *Private Eye*.

Ingrams, meanwhile, had become more interested in the theatre, having registered among others a memorable performance as a mad king in an open-air Oxford production of *Tamburlaine the Great*. Largely with his own capital he founded a travelling company called 'Tomorrow's Audience', the purpose being to tour schools, and by introducing children to professionally acted plays to increase in the next generation the very small percentage of the population that ever goes to the theatre. This was not a success, and was not helped by a flash manager in the habit of calling on impoverished headmasters in an enormous Jaguar sporting a large cigar.

That Was The Week That Was was just beginning, and Ingrams went so far as to write scripts for David Frost, only finally drawing the line when Frost insisted on continuing their discussion of some particular joke from inside the lavatory with the door open. Indeed this may, in some macabre sense, have been the Light on the Road to

Damascus: from then on Ingrams became increasingly concerned with *Private Eye*. Since then he has occasionally branched out into editing Cobbett or Beachcomber, writing about Malcolm Muggeridge or television, appearing as the scourge of Fleet Street on *What the Papers Say* or resident duffer on the News Quiz, but throughout the sixties he fiercely excluded work for anyone else as 'disloyal to the mag'.

The question everyone always used to ask about *Private Eye* at parties was whether the advertisements were genuine – various whores and perverts were found to be lurking about the columns of the magazine employing a variety of transparent and obscene codes to reach potential customers – and it reflected the confusion of readers who found themselves being consistently addressed in comic voices.

This 'comic voice' problem is one under which I have seen innocent visitors to the magazine physically crumple up. Finding themselves in a room full of people all imitating elderly clubmen and using this corporate fantasy as a vehicle from which to attack them, they very naturally feel themselves both victimised and excluded. It has been a habit with us all for years, and if Ingrams was not its initiator he has certainly always been a master of it. It served at the university as a defence against intellectual, emotional or political commitment – any statement made in a comic voice could carry the force of a straight statement but at the same time contained its own ejector seat if things got too hot – and it has become the style of a magazine.

There was, for years, a yellowing letter pinned to the board in Ingrams's office from Kenneth Tynan with the typewritten question, underlined, '*When are you going to get a point of view?*' A question that must have occurred to many *Private Eye* readers, particularly when a passionately embraced cause or even a passionately embraced public figure is suddenly subjected to a barrage of abuse or ridicule. If the comic voices, like the advertisements, are not real, what is the real voice of *Private Eye*, and more precisely of Richard Ingrams?

He is himself almost excessively reticent about his own

positive aims in the magazine, preferring to talk about 'producing a good gossip column, which is all that any newspaper can be' and dismissing any more explicit commitment as sentimental or 'boring'. But even a gossip column has its implicit political and social attitudes, and Ingrams's are as firmly and obstinately held as anybody's, subjected to little discussion, and defended, if it comes to the point, with a bellicose roar of 'Nonsense!'

The nearest I have ever heard him come to a confession of faith was in an interview once when he said that the single most important turning point in his life, apart from having to pay court to Frost on the lavatory seat, was failing his War Office Selection Board and having to do his National Service in the ranks. The Board was a barmy three-day charade inflicted on almost all ex public-school and grammar-school National Servicemen, consisting of a series of obstacle courses over which each individual was required at some point to lead the rest of the team. Those who passed went for three months to an Officer Cadet School at the end of their first year and spent the remainder of the two-year sentence tip-toeing about in flat hats, blushing to the roots of their hair every time they were saluted by a friend from school, and lolling about in the Officers' Mess learning to drawl like the Regulars. Ingrams for some reason failed it, and spent his time, where I saw him first, as a respected member of the Sergeants' Mess.

Translated into civilian terms, the Sergeants' Mess became the Pub. It is no coincidence that *Private Eye* has always been practically edited from a pub: first the Queen's Head and Eight Bells, on the corner of Cheyne Row near his family's old house in Chelsea, then a pub on the corner of Seven Dials, and now finally, even when he has given up drinking altogether, from the Coach and Horses on the corner of Greek Street and Romilly Street. Pubs, according to Ingrams, are where the Real People are: not plastic and Muzak pubs, not even journalists' pubs, but old-fashioned, beery, jolly Chestertonian pubs, with deaf, red-faced, porous-nosed old men in voluminous tweed caps and raincoats done up to the neck sitting in silence with an overflowing pint of mild, occasionally giving vent to some blinding obscenity about the weather or the party in power.

The pub allows a greater social mobility than, let us say, the drawing-room; but deaf, red-faced, porous-nosed old men in voluminous tweed caps are not in the end the wittiest of companions. *Private Eye*'s central institution, the Wednesday Lunch, soon moved to an upper room in the same pub. Admittedly the social mobility has rather been left behind with the beery old men, and there can be few drawing-rooms in London that are more exclusive: politicians, poets and famous names of show business, journalism and the criminal underworld all climb over one another for an invitation.

But the atmosphere is certainly more suitable to the exposition of Ingrams's patrician point of view, which Kenneth Tynan should have recognised, comic voices or no comic voices, seven years ago. It would be more accurate, really, to call it patrician prejudice, and it is a prejudice that the Sergeants' Mess and the Pub have only served to confirm: Royalty and the Aristocracy are obsessively comic, closely followed in order of absurdity by arrivistes, Jews, students, though not undergraduates, Africans, politicians, journalists, any other foreigners, pooves, women, and the working and the lower-middle classes. The greatest crime, because the most embarrassing, is Romantic Idealism, and the panacea Classical Moderation. To the core *Private Eye*, and Richard Ingrams, are British and Patrician.

It is in fact this identification of the Man with the Magazine that fills me with the greatest hope for Ingrams's future. He has placid depths, a familiar feature in Great Men, and used to spend long holidays in Scotland when we were at Oxford, 'rock-watching'. He is attractive to women. Candida Lycett-Green, then Candida Betjeman, once almost crashed her car during a driving lesson at the mere sight of his red sweater, and wrote a long, love-lorn lament on the subject in verse, which will no doubt one day be published. He himself adores nothing more passionately than the *status quo*. But he also inspires among men a savage personal loyalty that reduces contributors and friends to feudal vassals – even the most untameable gossip columnists on national newspapers – and he has created a very powerful position for himself and the magazine in English society.

Gladys

Lady Wilson, the poet, and wife of the former Prime Minister, gives the impression of being very shy – in our preliminary correspondence she said she doubted whether it was possible to get more than an impression of anyone in a single interview – and she has very pretty blue eyes that have a way of lingering a moment too long after she has answered a question: a look that combines candour, an irresistible desire to trust and be trusted and, at the same time, quiet reproof.

The fact that, throughout her time at Number Ten, Richard Ingrams and I had produced the fortnightly farrago of 'Mrs Wilson's Diary' in *Private Eye*, eventually turned into a knock-about West End show by Joan Littlewood, did not make that cool blue look any easier to bear.

In the Diary she appeared as a lovable, suburban, Wincarnis-tippling, ducks-up-the-wall innocent, naïvely observing the rum doings at Downing Street and constantly bursting into starry-eyed doggerel. When questioned about it by one newspaper she had said that if she ever met me she was going to bite me.

The first time I saw her talking about it on television I remember feeling guilty: the ducks-up-the-wall joke was obviously something she felt sensitive about, even though it seemed to fit her husband's bluff provincial presentation of himself and the facts of her own upbringing – the daughter of a poor Congregational minister, who still preserves a slight trace of her parents' Lancashire accent.

When they are in London, the Wilsons live now in a solidly opulent block of redbrick Edwardian flats across the road from Westminster Cathedral. A black daily with a reassuring smile showed me into a comfortably furnished drawing-room on the first floor. Any lingering dreams of the family enjoying a delicious bowl of Wholegerm Roughage Bricks in the dining area with Inspector

Trimfittering, or quaffing a tooth-mug of Wincarnis in front of the Kosiglow, evaporated. It could have been the home of any upper-middle class don with private means at one of the older universities: a few photographs in surprisingly small silver frames, well-polished furniture, a lot of new books still in their dust-jackets on broad white shelves, one or two small brightly-coloured primitive water-colours painted, as I discovered subsequently, by her father. Before I could notice any more, Mary Wilson came in.

It may be that in her public life she has acquired some mysterious invisible armour, but I had a strong sense that Royalty had entered the room.

She immediately did her best to put me at my ease, showing me the view from the window and expressing unexpectedly conservative reservations about the ecumenical impulse that had made the Anglican Church Commissioners give the land for the piazza to the Roman Catholic Cathedral. She has remained a staunch Congregationalist, even if the majority of her co-religionists have accepted amalgamation with the United Reformed Church. Harold himself has similar views and has always refused to read the lesson in church unless it was in the Authorised Version. We sat down on the sofa. Coffee was brought in modest white cups and the interview began.

Mary Wilson's *New Poems* consist of a central core dedicated to the memory of John Webster, a lifelong friend from Oxford who played the organ for the Wilsons' wedding at Mansfield College in 1940, as well as descriptive poems, landscapes from the Scilly Isles, a group of nursery pieces for her grandchildren, Catherine and Jennifer, a poetic exchange with her great friend, Sir John Betjeman – they met at the opera in 1966 – about their journey to the house in Diss where she was born, and various poems for special occasions. But the one that first caught my attention was *Mamzelle*, not only because it was a very sweet and truthful description of an innocent schoolgirl crush on the French Mistress –

> 'Pale skin, pink lips, a wide blue stare,
> Her page-boy fall of silky hair
> Swings on her shoulders like a bell . . .'

– but because it contained some lines that immediately brought to mind a picture of Mary Wilson herself, as John Betjeman would have loved her: a snub-nosed, sunburned sixteen-year-old in a gym-slip with the same blue eyes, looking eagerly out of the window of a hot class-room on a summer morning.

> 'The Summer Term had just begun;
> My desk was warm beneath the sun;
> I leaned across the window-ledge
> To smell the springing sweet-briar hedge . . .'

I asked her whether her schooldays had been as happy as they seemed. 'Oh yes, I was terribly happy there. Do you know the school?' I had to admit I didn't. 'It was called Milton Mount College. It's died now because it insisted on remaining independent after the war: it amalgamated with a school in Bournemouth called Wentworth, so now it's Wentworth Milton Mount.'

She had pulled a photograph album with tissue paper between the pages across the glass coffee-table and opened it at a picture of the school: a massive, late-Victorian country house in Sussex, with white-painted window-frames – 'That was the room where I slept, there, looking out over the lake' – and a heavy, pillared portico. 'It belonged to the Montefiore family and was opened as a school by Dame Margaret Lloyd George. It was for ministers' daughters: well actually it was about half-and-half, the fees of the children who weren't ministers' daughters paid for those who were, and I had a bursary there. It was a most beautiful house.'

More photographs: a long table laid with a white cloth and water-jugs, the light from the windows beyond reflected in the polished floor, a vast hall with dark panelling and plaster mouldings. 'There's the Ben Greet Company that used to come down and do plays for us. That's all the girls round the Round Pond. We were saving up for a swimming-pool which we never actually got when I was there, but they got one later on. This was the Assembly Hall – that was gold-leaf, and this was all silk damask. The story was that the family had it all done up like that for a visit by Edward VII, and then he never came.'

I asked her if she had been a prefect at the school. 'No, no. I wasn't' – a chuckle – 'I'm not the prefect type. Too dreamy. They said, "*Oh*, she's *so* dreamy: a dreamer round the place." But I don't know how to describe it: it was like a boy's boarding-school. I was terribly lucky going to a marvellous place like that. Unfortunately it spoilt me for real life.'

Real life, in which she became so closely involved, has demolished Milton Mount – 'I went down there a couple of weeks ago, actually, and had a look at it: they've pulled down the building and built a block of flats. Some of the grounds are still there.' But in her dream, preserved in verse, the house still stands, her desk is still warm in the morning sun and, in her loving memory of it, she has even provided the swimming-pool they couldn't afford:

> 'The sunny days are hurrying past;
> Their painful sweetness will not last;
> The poppies burn among the hay,
> The heartless cuckoo sings all day;
> The Home Farm woods are green and cool,
> There's laughter from the swimming-pool
> At end-of-term I say farewell
> For ever, to Mamzelle . . .'

I asked her if poetry had been an escape from real life in times of unhappiness. 'No, I mostly go and pray then. I try not to bludgeon God with requests but I do find it helps to have a good pray.' The cool blue look. 'And also you dismiss the periods of your life when you aren't happy from your mind. You literally forget them. But I do think about the happy times. Nostalgia has laid its dead hand on me all my life. What was it John Betjeman said about it? "People talk about nostalgia as if it was an illness, like neuralgia."' Mary Wilson seems to feel they may be right: as she says in a poem addressed *To Nostalgia*:

> '. . . That, in the magic of your spell, I may
> Have lived my muddled life in retrospect;
> And I am troubled by the fact that I
> Like Lot's wife, looking back, may petrify.'

But her dreams aren't only about the past: they are also

about what might have been. The childhood illness that made her parents decide to take her away from the village school at the age of twelve and send her as a boarder to Milton Mount – 'I don't know, I got thinner and thinner and paler and paler, they never did discover what it was' – also meant that she missed a year's work that she never succeeded in catching up. 'The only thing I really worked at was English. I had dropped Latin in my first year because I just couldn't cope with it, so I didn't get to university, because I had to have Latin. And that was the great regret of my life.'

Hence, presumably, the added attraction when she married Harold, of his being a don at Oxford, and Oxford recurs more than once in the poems. In real life, she has the consolation of a son, Robin, who now works for the Open University and lives and studies there, and she remembers life in Oxford at the end of the war – Kenneth Tynan striding about in his cloak and holding forth in Fuller's, undergraduates making bonfires of furniture in the High and burning effigies of Hitler and Mussolini – with obvious pleasure. But going back to her own phrase 'my muddled life', I asked her whether at that point she'd imagined she was going to be a don's wife for good. The cool blue look. 'Yes.' So everything that happened subsequently was rather a surprise? An even longer look. 'Yes.'

It would be easy to leave the impression there: a sweet, sad nature, reluctantly swept into the rough world of politics, seeking consolation in prayer and pleasure in writing poetry. But there is also the well-armoured public figure I was aware of when she first entered the room. 'I don't think I'd want to harp too much on the life as a don's wife because, after all, it was a long time ago and we had a long apprenticeship in politics before Harold got to Number Ten. I was a Minister's wife when the children were growing up: people seem to imagine I suddenly *leapt*' – a chuckle – 'from a suburb *straight* to Number Ten.'

Feeling that we were going to have to talk about 'Mrs Wilson's Diary' sooner or later – in which she had figured as the heroine 'Gladys' – I asked her why she had agreed to give me an interview, the first of its kind for five years. The

93

longest look of all. 'Because I always believe in meeting the enemy face to face.

'No, you got me all wrong. You see, I'll tell you this: we have *one* bottle of HP Sauce a year, if that. I have *never* tasted Wincarnis wine. I am *not* a suburban woman. I have lived all over the country. And she was such a *silly* woman, laughing about everything and dancing about and being so excited with everything. It wasn't me.'

Even as I squirmed I couldn't help realising, for the first time, how difficult her position must have been. What we had in fact got right was Harold's assumed public image – the pipe and the pint of beer – rather than the private cigars and brandy. How could she possibly have defended herself as she does now when that image was so important? She seemed to sense that and shifted her ground.

'Well, all right "Mrs Wilson's Diary" was a joke and, after all, I used to read it and think what you'd described wasn't nearly as bizarre as it really was. I could have told you some things which were much funnier. But it was the *snobbish* element I didn't like. Because if I *had* drunk gallons of Wincarnis wine and poured HP Sauce over everything it wouldn't have *mattered*. And I don't think it's very funny,' referring to our current sequel in *Private Eye*, 'Dear Bill' – 'all this about Mr Thatcher, poor chap.

'Why make fun? I wasn't brought up to make fun of people. And I don't think it's very nice. All right, if you can't stand the heat keep out of the kitchen and all that, but then one is *in* the kitchen because one happens to be involved with the person that's doing the job.'

Nevertheless public life, she admits, has had its compensations: 'Meeting Neil Armstrong, for instance, was a terrific thrill for me – actually to meet the man that stood on the moon. There was a poem about that in my first book, *Selected Poems*. I asked him what the earth looked like, and he said it was an enormous great shining orb and you could see all the countries. I didn't realise that the earth would shine but he said it was brighter than any full moon you could imagine and much bigger: this enormous great shining orb. And meeting Auden, too. John Webster took me to have coffee with him one morning in Oxford.'

And, if she didn't actually keep a diary, she did make time to write poetry, particularly at Chequers. 'One was waited on hand and foot down there. Lovely smells: polished wood, flowers, lots of box hedges.'

There was the other side, of course. 'When we were fighting an election, for instance, the car used to draw up and I would get out first: there'd be arc-lights and I couldn't see a thing, you could just hear cheers and howls. You never knew if you were going to get something thrown at you. I've been spat on, had flour thrown, all those sorts of things. But somehow you got used to it. It was part of the job and you did it. One became hardened, I suppose. But it doesn't mean it hurts any the less.'

But now the satire and flood-lights and fair-weather friends – she and Giles used to keep a list of people who asked them out to dinner when they were in power and entirely ignored them when they weren't – have receded, and even politics seem less in the foreground of her life. We met, by coincidence, on May 14, the TUC's not entirely successful Day of Action. I asked if she had any qualms about us both working. A moment's thought, as if it hadn't crossed her mind. 'No.' She laughed, again I thought like a girl let out from school, and told me a story about a woman she'd met that morning who worked at the Army & Navy Stores and who had said that beating the strike brought out the best in us. 'I didn't tell her that the people she was fighting were actually her fellow human beings. But from the political point of view, I don't know enough about it to give an opinion.' Did she actually persuade Harold to resign? 'No, no, I didn't. But I'm not going to say I was sorry when he did.'

Her time now seems to be spent mainly with her grandchildren, when she's not writing, and in charitable work. 'I do a certain amount for spastics, a certain amount for the blind – but no more than anybody else.' Even in private life, though, she still claims to be delighted when people recognise Harold in the street and not her, or when, on the famous trip to Diss, the same thing happened with Sir John:

> 'Now, as we stroll beside the Mere,
> Reporters suddenly appear;

> You draw a crowd of passers-by
> Whilst I gaze blandly at the sky . . .'

'How can I put it? I *am* reserved and I wish people well, but let them leave me alone to get on with my life. Praise *and* blame embarrass me. Slightly.'

So why court publicity by exposing her soul in poetry? 'I don't know. The first book I wrote for myself, but I was terribly pleased to have it published because – how can I explain it? – everybody who writes likes to see their stuff in print. I thought, whether anybody reads it or not, provided the publisher doesn't lose money – that's my non-conformist attitude coming out – provided he got his return, then *this was my book*. You see the big hurdle I had was that people would think it was "because". "Oh well of course . . ." Which is *true*. After all, the publishers naturally would publish stuff written by the Prime Minister's wife. But I don't want to be patted on the head and have people say, "There, there. Nice little poems." I really don't know. I write because I must write, I publish because I must publish.' She says she welcomes criticism and I believe her. She read extensively as a child – her father's faded collection of Collins' Classics are still up there on the shelf sandwiched between Harold's review copies – and quotes Tennyson with the enjoyment of a gourmet remembering a menu. She is therefore aware that her poems are full of resonances of the nineteenth century. 'You've certainly got to be careful of echoes. I remember I had a marvellous line and then, suddenly – and I can't remember ever reading that particular sonnet before – I came across the same line, and that really upset me. I have a friend who's an American poet and she said, "I try to copy John Betjeman as well as I can." And I said, "Oh dear! The thing is to try not! Having done all the reading, to try not." '

There is also the problem of metre. I risked taking her up on what I thought was an uneven line in a poem called *The Old Woman of Peckham*, a lonely old pensioner talking:

'Mother, come with us to New Zealand!'

Mary Wilson took the book and tried it again, testing the

stress on different words: ' "Mother, *come* with us to New Zealand." It seemed right at the time. "Mother, come *with us* to New Zealand." Yes, I agree that's wrong. But gosh, yes: there's 9, 7, 9, 7, and then a 10 comes along. You try to work it out like that. Try to be meticulous.

'I also find it difficult not to make *lists* in my poems. I think "That's another list." With *The Opening of Parliament* I tried to get it all in but I never got the tiaras in, because "tiaras" just doesn't scan, so I had to leave them out. I had to put "costly jewellery", which I didn't like. If I had my choice I would get rid of "costly" because it's not a good word. But I couldn't get the tiaras in, no matter how much I tried. That was a poem commissioned by Penguin, though, for a book of poetry about the Queen, to a given subject, and that's much more difficult I think. That's why the poor Laureate must find it so hard.'

Normally though, the emotion and the sound of a line come first. In Scilly, where she is happiest, she gets up at six – 'I'm a lark, that's why I think I was sometimes a bit lethargic at late-night receptions at Number Ten. I can only write first thing in the morning when my brain is clear, and I work till about eleven.' At a window again, as she did as a girl, composing, correcting, putting them away in a drawer – 'I find they generally take about three months to gel' – and counting out the rhythm until she is satisfied.

She is a little more defensive about owning up to any autobiographical content. 'People had a good go at all the love poems in the first book and they said "Who was it?" and "Who did you mean in this?" I said to them, "I wrote a poem when I was at school called *The Murderer's Wife* and that didn't necessarily make me a murderer's wife." '

But the armour is not very thick. We talked about some lines from a poem called *Manic-depressive*:

> 'I should like to dig a deep, dark hole
> And lie down in it, as if in my bed,
> And to stretch up high and blot out the sky,
> As I pull the grasses over my head . . .'

At first she said it was written for a doctor friend, now dead, 'as a joke'. 'He thought it was very funny. It was exaggerated. We all feel a bit like that. I wouldn't like to

97

think I really am a manic-depressive though.' A pause again, as she thought about it. 'You may not think it, but I am terribly thin-skinned and I try to preserve a façade of dignity and calm. Because I am very arrogant and proud and not really sweet at all. I am arrogant, proud, independent . . . and, sometimes, bloody-minded. And if anything happens, that I'm embarrassed about, I wouldn't let anyone see. And, as far as that poem goes, I have a very clear mental image of actually *digging* a hole, climbing down into it and *pulling* the earth over my head. It's very clear. And I suppose you could call it a death-wish. But it's more wanting to hide.'

That seemed to express the contradiction between public and private life more clearly than I could have done and, remembering the impression she had made on me when she first came into the room, I understood the memory of Balmoral – another positive perk of the years in office – at the end of *The Opening of Parliament*:

> 'A small quick figure, walking all alone
> Across a glen studded with standing deer.
> She notes a crumbling wall, an open gate,
> With countrywoman's eyes she views the scene;
> Yet, walking free upon her own estate
> Still, in her solitude, she is the Queen.'

But even the Royal 'We-are-not-amused' response to all the years of cheek conceals a weakness for a joke. Our discussion of the 'Diary' had ended, on her side, very severely: 'Why make fun? I wasn't brought up to make fun of people, and I don't think it's very nice.' Just before I left, she mentioned the television programme *Yes, Minister*. 'I don't know whether you watch that – I think it's so marvellous!' Surely she objected on principle: the programme was, after all, making fun? 'No, because it's making fun of civil servants.' She laughed almost louder than I did. 'Oh dear . . .' I asked her to think of the poor civil servants howling with grief in doorways all along Whitehall. She was still laughing. 'My heart bleeds for them.'

Cracking Jokes

The Great Illusionist

Haroldini is now generally acknowledged to be the greatest stage magician of the twentieth century, and despite the unfortunate publicity that surrounded his recent voluntary retirement there are many grateful fans who will welcome the first volume of his autobiography, *Some of the People*, published this week by the Official Receiver at £15.75. Here at last Haroldini reveals fully and frankly the almost incredible amount of hard work, rigorous self-discipline and quiet piety that lay behind the carefree façade: the heartbreak and agony behind those dazzlingly successful tricks that kept audiences gurgling with pleasure, all through the Silly Sixties and into the Serious Seventies.

In those madcap, romantic days of Dr Barnard and the mini-skirt, of the Moonrocket and the Third Programme, it was fashionable to feel sorry for Haroldini's comic stooge, 'Mr Edward', a plummy-voiced duffer with a happy knack of mishandling every trick he attempted. Eggs broke in his pockets, cards fell from his sleeves, and water flooded from his hat whenever he raised it. It was only years later that 'Mr Edward' admitted to having been a fun-loving millionaire playboy all the time who had only acted out his part in order to gratify a secret lust for humiliation. Now, with the publication of Haroldini's own story, it is clear that those sympathies were entirely misplaced: it was the magician himself, and not his infinitely sophisticated stooge, that we should have felt sorry for.

Few who saw him will ever forget the round-shouldered lope on to the stage, the black top hat spinning on a white-gloved finger, the silver hair glinting in the spotlight, the long starched cuffs and the flying black tails: then the bewildering succession of tricks, while 'Mr Edward' stood gloomily on one side of the stage, breaking the eggs, losing his cards or soaking himself with water. Haroldini would stand in a blur of coloured scarves and white handkerchiefs, white doves inexplicably fluttering from his coat, rabbits pulled pink-eyed and twitching from the hat, full packs of cards shuffling themselves effortlessly into his outspread palm, jugs of milk arching out and splashing into paper hats only to be crumpled to nothing and vanish. Then 'Mr Edward' would break another egg, and the audience would rise and cheer.

And yet, all the time, we now learn, the great Haroldini was going through moral agony. Indeed, the more they cheered, the more he suffered. As a child, he tells us, he always shunned the limelight, and studied late into the night, barefoot and shivering in the flickering glow of a single candle, to prepare himself for a responsible self-effacing role in the running of the country. He writes movingly of the summer evening when, as a boy of five, he was first tempted to entertain and impress an elderly aunt who refused to take his political ideas seriously and kept putting him on her lap and tickling him.

'I suppose I was desperately anxious to engage her attention on more important matters, and I remember, almost without thinking, that I took three thimbles from Mother's workbasket and the dried pea out of Grannie's whistle. I asked my aunt to watch carefully, and to tell me which thimble covered the pea. In a matter of moments she was fascinated, and I was able to explain to her in very simple terms why she was unwise to trust either the Conservative or the Liberal party to maintain the value of her tiny pension. Since then I have been under constant pressure, throughout my life, to develop dexterity and agility at the expense of tough-minded application and steadfastness.

'There have been times, and I will be absolutely frank about this, when I have longed to go to the footlights and say to the people quite openly: "Look, this top hat is not empty as it may appear; it has little springs all round the inside containing coloured handkerchiefs. Look at this wretched rabbit stuck away in a secret pocket in the seat of my trousers, look at these pathetic doves trussed up under my armpits: they do not really appear by magic, it is all a rotten trick designed to make you part with your money. Let us sit down together and talk about the ultimate verities!" But economic pressures have never allowed it, and I have been forced to continue this idiot charade. There have been times too when I prayed that my touch would desert me, that I might be permitted to break one egg, to put my hand into the hat and bring it out holding nothing. But even this has been denied me.'

All this, of course, does much to explain the more 'political' tricks of the later years like the Vanishing Incomes Policy, and their growing savagery in the case of the American-inspired Indochinese Human Torch trick and the original Sawing a Biafran in Half, both of which were frequently fatal. It also explains the darkness which in later years seems to have descended on his mind. If only, one feels, looking at the airily smiling, magically successful performer pictured on the back of the book, so bravely concealing his secret despair, if only he'd told us he wanted to be a politician: what great things he might have achieved!

Not My Day

An annoying start. My Teasmade, set to go off as per usual at 7 am, turned out to be minus the teapot part. As a result, on the stroke of seven, the light came on, the buzzer went off, and the bloody thing poured scalding hot water all over my new marquetry top bedside table from Heal's, absolutely soaking my foam rubber posture pillow, and ruining my newly laundered Rear Admiral brushed nylon pyjamas. I was hopping mad, I don't mind admitting.

To crown it all, Bob Carr chose precisely that moment to come barging straight in to my holy of holies, as I refer to my tastefully decorated bachelor suite at Number Ten – with its nautical blue ceiling designed by Madge Thrower, its Hokusai Shimbun multi-output loudspeaker equipment, and the *Quaint Moments in Old London* series of art repro copper engravings by Melvyn Pymm – saying he had to see me on urgent business.

He seemed, however, hugely amused by the Teasmade having gone wrong, and said, 'Ha ha. I always said you'd get into hot water one of these days, living alone like this.'

I said, 'Shut up, you bloody fool. Get a mop and start swabbing up.' He then replied: 'It's no good, Fatty, it is your own fault for not getting a proper gentleman's gentleman to boil your water in the mornings, thus dramatically reducing unemployment on Tyneside and elsewhere at a stroke. As it is, on your own head be it.'

I refused to be stung by this, and said, 'Nonsense. I already have Mrs Behr once a day.' I then pointed to the Teasmade and added: 'If you are incapable of absorbing the inevitable redundancies occasioned by the introduction of more complex technology, I for one am not surprised that people throw rotten cabbages whenever you show your silly bloody face in public. But come to the point. What is it you wish to see me about? I am a busy man.'

He said, 'Curly Barber and I dreamed up a little wheeze at Crockford's last night.'

'Very well,' I replied coldly. 'Leave it on the occasional table by the Elisabeth Frink and get out.' With this, I turned angrily on my heel and flounced out into the bathroom to do my Egyptian Air Force exercises.

While performing the 'Stand on Your Own Foot' exercise, I unfortunately fell over, banging my head on the Sèvres bidet presented to me last year by Monsieur Pompadour. I also had to get out of the bath on several occasions, first to turn off the *Today* programme, which seemed to be concerned exclusively with destruction in Ulster, and subsequently to adjust the manual control on my Banzai Shinto turntable, which repeatedly became stuck in Arturo Blitzkrieg's *sostenuto* during the famous fiddling scene from *Il Inflammazione de Nero*.

After perusing the contents of my Red Boxes, which contained over a hundred old restaurant bills submitted by Reggie Maudling for expenses, a 'saucy' postcard from Ian Smith and a curious ticking parcel which, unwrapped, appeared to be some sort of home-made wireless set, I breakfasted as usual off one slice of starch-reduced Slimmawheet with a scrape of Blue Band and a cup of unsweetened black Kardomah coffee, and went down to the Cabinet Room to look at oilskins in the new catalogue from Simpson's.

As I watched my colleagues coming into the Cabinet Room (at present being treated again for dry rot by white-overalled workmen from the Ministry of the Environment, some of whom speak fluent Russian) I was overwhelmed, as I always am, by a sense of my own superiority. They are a shabby lot, and it is a source of pride to me that I have risen above them. To pass the time until they settled down, I cast my eye over the note left by Bob Carr. It was written, rather unsteadily, on the back of a ticket for somewhere called the Nudes-a-Gogo Club, and bore the words 'Final Solution'.

I asked Barber what they meant by this when he and Carr came in, and they explained that the ideal population of the United Kingdom, in the interests of efficiency and the satisfactory running of service industries to maintain a reasonable standard of living for the nation's supertax-payers, was ten million. The remaining surplus, which could be statistically broken down into Communist agitators, scroungers, immigrants, children, lunatics and old people, should be 'shaken out'.

Gavin Pine, our PR adviser, had apparently come up with some cliff-hanger scheme of the type used at Brussels and in Salisbury, whereby the general public is to be kept in suspense over the eventual cost to the taxpayer of the 'shaking out' plant, to be supplied by Porton Down, until such time as the necessary legislation is passed. I said the plan sounded perfectly fair to me, and the Cabinet dispersed.

I just had time for a cheese salad and a glass of water for lunch, prepared by Mrs Behr, before dashing off to catch the 1.43 to Broadstairs, leaving Alec to deal with Question Time.

After an extremely disagreeable trip down in the train, throughout which I was pestered by a plump matron in her mid-forties with pebble spectacles who kept asking me whether I wanted to play doctors and nurses, I arrived home to find that Dad had fallen off the roof trying to attach a pro Common Market banner to the television aerial, and broken several ribs. This was a nuisance as it made me late for sailing.

However, as I said to Captain Marryat, the horny-handed old salt who works, or should I say worked, the steering thing at the back end of *Morning Cloud*, watching the lights of Broadstairs disappear into the dusk, it's the little mishaps in life that really make one laugh in the long run. I was, in fact, just having a good laugh, when the main upright thing began vibrating, came loose from its socket, and fell over, unfortunately killing him. This delayed me for a further forty-five minutes, and I was not in my suspended bed, off Cherbourg, for the start of the Millionaires' Handicap, until 10 pm. As I said to begin with, it was not my day.

After the Staggers

THE NS EDITORSHIP

Applications are invited for the post of
Editor of the NEW STATESMAN. Anthony
Howard, the present editor, has held the
position for nearly six years, since May
1972, and is intending to leave in the spring
of next year.

Applications from both men and women
should be sent to the General Manager
NEW STATESMAN, 10 Great Turnstile, London WC1V 7HJ to arrive by 12 January
1978.

Chatsworth
Derbyshire
11 January, 1978

Dear Whoever It May, as they say, Concern!

You must think me an utter prune writing to you *absolutely*
out of the blue like this, particularly on such a blush-
making shade of lilac paper embossed with the ducal
coronet, but my husband Dickie is *quite* fanatical about his
boring old shooting, and one has once again been *dragged*
along. I am told our hostess, Debo Devonshire, has a
mildly Left-wing sister – I think she may be called Jessica –
but one hasn't dared mention it for fear of being thought a
harbourer of Reds under the Bed, something Dickie
himself has rather tended to go on about over the years.

The thing is, would I do?

What *emboldened* me, as Dickie's dirty uncle Horace always used to say – I don't know whether you ever met him but he was the *most* frightful pouncer in taxis, particularly on one – was the phrase 'applications from both men *and women*'. Gosh, you are good. How many papers can one think of, in these grisly unisex days of Equal Opportunities and all the balls and blather one reads about having to be sexually undiscriminating, that would actually take the trouble to make one feel *really* feminine? I suppose that's what one's always so adored about the New Staggers: a sort of cosy old-fashioned respect for the things that matter.

Is there *any* chance, do you think, of one's having a crack at editing the Mag? A few years ago, of course, it would have been out of the question: one obviously adored having the children, but somehow one was always talking to nannies and boarding schools and one never seemed to have a second to oneself. Now they're off one's hands, so to speak, there does seem to be so much more time: friends, very *close* friends especially, are always on at one to get a job or do *something*, and having a little paper to edit did strike one as being *just* what the doctor ordered.

God knows, one cares enough about the issues of the day, as do, obviously, your *tremendously* talented team of writers, from the tough and jolly courageous political comment at the front to whoever it is compiles those columns of *heart-rending* appeals from lonely upper-middle-class intellectuals at the back. What is more – and this does seem to me essential for anyone, man or woman, who is going to take on a responsible job, which editing the *New Statesman* is, whatever people may say about the Sunday papers eroding its circulation, it's still enormously influential, particularly with people like oneself – one *is* in a position, though one dreads to blow one's own trumpet, to influence events in one's own tiny way.

Only the other night, to give you a case in point, I found myself having dinner next to the Persian Ambassador, *the* most divine little man with very pretty eyes, and, my dear, one absolutely *flew* at him over the caviar. I think he'd brought it himself, and it was quite delicious, perfectly complemented by the Puligny Montrachet, enormous

106

glinting black globules so delicate they broke impercept-ibly between the teeth, like sucking dried flakes of sea-salt from a fisherman's armpit, and yet one couldn't allow oneself to be gagged. One went doggedly on, through the Filet de Boeuf en Croûte with quite a good Latour to the Crêpes Suzette and Yquem, until one was absolutely convinced to one's own satisfaction that all the stories of the Shah's political opponents being tortured and starved to death were, as he finally confessed, 'very exaggerated'.

Now I realise that there's more to being editor of the *New Statesman* than that, although I've often seen both my – dare I say it – predecessors – there, I have – putting in noble work at some jolly stuffy dinner parties. She must, clearly, have a real rapport with her contributors. And here again, I suppose, one is in a privileged position: I can't think of a single regular contributor to the Staggers, with the possible exception of Mr Arthur Marshall, who is, I am told, rather *outré* in his more-proletarian-than-thou atti-tude, that I haven't got to know socially, and in some cases *intimately*.

I've always found them quite enchanting, thoughtful and well-mannered, always telling one *fascinating* bits of gossip about the inner working of the Labour Party, and I've come to feel over the years that I'm someone with whom they know they can really let their back hair down and spill the beans.

There is of course the hurdle of what is called a Strong Editorial Line – I don't mean insisting on them handing in their work on time: I've always assumed that Tony and Paul (Johnson) had some sort of Hudson figure behind the green baize door who did the badgering on that – and when I was talking to my hairdresser about it, that aspect did preoccupy us for some time. He had *marvellous* ideas for bringing it closer to the ordinary man and woman in the street by giving it a sort of *Woman's Realm* coloured cover with perhaps a picture of Audrey Callaghan in a chunky-knit sweater on the front, but the Strong Editorial Line problem stumped us.

And then, you know, it suddenly struck me under the drier that perhaps a Strong Editorial Line *may* in the past have been more trouble than it was worth. I remember when Tony H. suddenly took one and attacked little Wilson, everyone thought he'd either gone mad or was making a last-ditch attempt to increase the circulation, and Paul J.'s campaign to get readers to follow his example and have their buttons sewn on after the Grosvenor Square riots by waiters at the Ritz never seemed to catch on somehow, simply because the average Staggers reader couldn't afford it, even then, when the Double Christmas Issue didn't cost ten bob.

Indeed, it occurs to me that the economic factor might, after all, be one's strongest card. I agree the Gay Hussar is one of the best restaurants in London, if not in the world, but for editorial lunches wouldn't it make more sense financially if you were to let Paolo and Francesca rustle you something up *chez nous* in Eaton Square? If it's too far from Great Turnstile, why not move over lock, stock and barrel? There's masses of room, and I think we could probably run to fresh flowers beside every typewriter and someone to change the ashtrays. And of course there is always Keepings for the weekends. I know Dickie's shooting friends would be tickled pink. Is my proposal too *crassly* revolutionary? What I'm offering, I suppose, is somewhere where you all would feel *at home*.

As always,
Flora Glossop.

No Alternative

A Union Jack in snow white, blood red and vivid navy blue fills the screen, fluttering and snapping in a stiff breeze: then, to the distant strains of a Thirties-style German march and the insistent chanting of a hundred thousand voices 'Thatch-er! Thatch-er! Thatch-er!' the Face of the Leader is superimposed on the flag, her upper lip lifted in a smile. Over this, the title in Daily Telegraph *Bold Gothic – 'THE TORY WAY, PART XVI: EDUCATION'.*

A sudden roar of merriment, and the screen is filled with porous-nosed revellers in three-piece suits and upswept moustaches, swaying to and fro in a state of reckless inebriation. Some, shorter, balder, and more melancholy, seem unsteady on their feet, and liable at any moment to be borne under by the crush. Others, heavier and more energetic, haul themselves hand over hand across mountainous, garishly-painted Tory ladies of the night. A caption 'The El Piranha Rooms, Hendon'. Tousled, slightly the worse for wear, but otherwise the perfect matinée idol, Education Minister Marsh Carlsberg de L'Isle fights his way towards the camera and treats us to a view of his bridgework.

CARLSBERG: Society. Well, to be more precise, the North Hendon Used Car Dealers' Artistic Appreciation Society. (*Beer cascades over his head, cries of 'Sorry old chummy', etc.*) But typical of the Tory Society we pledged ourselves at the last election (*inaudible witticisms and cheers*) to protect and to foster. Because – make no mistake about it – this society is a fragile and sophisticated one (*eighteen-stone barmaid passed over the heads of the crowd smiling at camera*) that is constantly under threat. It is the purpose of this series of films to identify that threat, wheresoever it may come from. (*Looks fiercely into camera, then consults small bald reveller who has appeared*

109

under his armpit.) Was that all right? (*Reveller collapses, but there are reassuring cries of 'Bloody terrific, Minister, have another one!' from off-screen.*)

We find ourselves at floor level, menaced by several hundred babies of various races, predominantly white, dribbling and puking their way towards us across the floor of a recently vandalised hospital. A caption: 'THEM'. Threatening chords, the film slowed down to emphasise the mood of horror. Carlsberg's voice is heard off.

CARLSBERG (*off*): Every day, the little creatures in this one room alone consume enough carbohydrates to supply the El Piranha Rooms, Hendon, with potato crisps for a full six minutes. Do not be deceived: these are not babies in the sense that we Tories know them – pink, self-reliant, responsible little citizens being carried past by the au pair girl at drinks time. These are clinging, work-shy layabouts, in many cases unable to stand on their own feet, a permanent drain on taxpayers' money that could be spent on lining up the gin-and-tonics on the bar at the El Piranha Rooms, Hendon, and creating more wealth in the private sector. What is worse, they expect to be educated. And that is where I come in . . .

A door opens at the far end of the room. Carlsberg enters, wearing a gas-mask and protective rubber clothing, and wades purposefully towards us.

. . . They are not prepared to contribute funds, pay for their round, except in terms of Income Tax which is vitally needed to pay for incentives to Big Earners. Which is why, as a Conservative, I have to put my foot down.

Puts foot down, strangled cries from the floor.
A fruit barrow, with bewhiskered spiv. Caption: 'An Educationalist in the Market Place'.

ROGUE-BYCESON: 'Ullo. My old china Marsh Carlsberg de L'Isle has set us a bit of a poser there. Only so many bites to be had at the old teacher's apple. Fair's fair, those bites must go to those who can afford them. (*Polishes Golden Delicious on sleeve, demolishes it with three gargantuan chomps, tosses apple-core over shoulder and chokes, remainder of speech incomprehensible.*)

We discover Carlsberg in front of a blackboard. Caption: 'The Commercial Sector'. Various public schoolboys loaf about in attitudes of nervous exhaustion, puffing at cigarettes and studying colour brochures advertising the El Piranha Rooms, Hendon.

CARLSBERG: Thank you, Rogue-Byceson. It is for this reason that we plan to introduce the idea of Student Loans. By borrowing the money to attend schools like this – in view of necessary cut-backs in the state sector, probably more like this (*caption sequence shows views of vandalised comprehensive recently gutted by fire*) – the student will no longer represent a drain at any stage – urchin, boot-boy or young hooligan – on the pockets of responsible members of our society.

A brief glimpse of the El Piranha Rooms, where revelry is on the increase and champagne is being opened. Then the outside of an Employment Exchange, where Rogue-Byceson stands muffled against the cold in front of shivering queue.

ROGUE-BYCESON: In the present somewhat bracing economic climate, you may be wondering, how is the student, on completion of his studies, going to pay us back if he cannot find the kind of cushy number in which to get up to the usual union high-jinks?

Exterior Wormwood Scrubs. Carlsberg pushes open studded wooden door.

CARLSBERG: Conservatives have thought about that. Already dramatic reductions have been made in the prison population, much of which has been reabsorbed into our society – in most cases the North Hendon UCDAAS – in anticipation of the influx of young bankrupts. No Tory Government, however, is going to tolerate the burden of keeping these work-shy monkeys in luxury for the rest of their lives. They will be re-educated for useful work – probably behind the bar at the El Piranha Rooms, Hendon – securing yet another vital Tory economy. By the end of the century we hope to have wound up the whole education racket entirely.

We return to the El Piranha Rooms, Hendon, where various distinguished academics in broad arrows and manacles are seen serving shorts before the chandelier collapses under the weight of revelry. Caption: 'The Tory Way – You Know It Makes Sense', patriotic music and slow fade to black.

The Queue of Hearts

The story so far: Chanticleer Bogart, whose victory in a by-election at Sowersby North brought about by the death of his mother Lady Pneumonia Bogart who had represented the consituency for Labour for the last thirty years (in a shoot-out with the Town Clerk Jasper T. Pureheart over a question of building contracts) has brought him to Westminster at the age of nineteen, is deeply shocked when a member of the Labour Cabinet asks him to become more than his PPS. *Now read on*:

Chanticleer's emerald eyes, a shade paler than the green leather of the back benches and flecked with traces of pure gold, widened in disbelief. It was, as he ascertained from a glance at the wafer-thin Beaune-L'Escroc gold wrist-watch his mother had given him, almost three o'clock in the afternoon, and of the six other Members of Parliament present, five were asleep. Horace Micklethwaite, a former used-car salesman now serving the Labour interest in the West Country, was the only one awake. Standing by the Dispatch Box in a slanting beam of sunlight that fell, a-dance with busy motes in the dry, stale air of the Chamber, from a window high above the deserted Strangers' Gallery, he presented an unattractive sight: the moist gleam of his bald head, the brown, close-set eyes under the thick black fur of his eyebrows, that possessed, like his square-cut black moustache, the consistency of old horsehair stuffing, the two-inch gap in his upper teeth, all filled Chanticleer with a vague sense of disquiet.

It wasn't what he was saying: at least Chanticleer didn't think it was. In the absence of the official Government Spokesman for the Ministry of Defence he appeared to be presenting a Bill for the retrospective acceptance of an EEC Decree for the metrication of containers of bubonic plague bacillus destined for use in maintaining Internal Security. Certainly nothing that Chanticleer's friend Andrew, the political correspondent of *Knitting Today*, would have urged him to be present at if he was interested in building a career in politics.

But looking round him now, as his slumbering colleagues allowed the air to escape rhythmically, and sometimes in sharper, deeper, more resonant tuba-notes from their flaccid bodies, he wasn't sure he wanted to build a career in politics after all.

The measured striking of Big Ben interrupted him in these thoughts, and his eye lighted on the Royal Cipher, glowing red and blue and gold above the gently snoring Speaker. The crown, supported by its two heraldic beasts, seemed almost to become radiant as the great clock boomed the first stroke of the hour, filling all the air around it with pulses of a divine presence, and Chanticleer was transported in fancy into another world.

A better, purer world, where all men dwelt together in peace under the gentle sway of a Virgin Queen: a woman, like his own mother perhaps, whose lightest frown was enough to bring the most unruly of her subjects to order and repentance, and whose sweet smile was the best and most treasured reward for industry, or gallantry or spiritual endeavour.

Chanticleer was woken from this reverie by a trombone-slide of flatulence that seemed to have escaped its author without waking him, and found the benches filling with what could have been the contents of any provincial public house at closing time. He looked down at his Order Paper and saw the cause: a Private Member's Bill at half-past three seeking to introduce compulsory cosmetic eye-surgery for all immigrants from the Colony of Hong Kong, that Andrew of *Knitting Today* had ringed in red as a 'corker'.

Then, across a now crowded Chamber, Chanticleer saw her! Margaret, Margaret T. . . . Whether it was the hint of blue-silver in her immaculately lacquered hair, or the deliberate grace of her deportment as she made her way to her accustomed place on the Opposition Front Bench, Chanticleer would never know.

All he was aware of was his heart, that beat against his ribs like a bird beating its wings against the bars of a cage. His cupid's bow of a mouth half opened in consternation, and his emerald eyes followed her, worshipping.

She sat, crossed one exquisite silk-stockinged leg over the other and then drew down the perfectly sewn hem of her skirt to conceal a knee so lovely in its undimpled innocence that a gasp sprang unbidden to his lips. What was this seething in his veins? What did it mean, this racing of his pulses, this dizziness that seized him? The whole scene before him became transmuted by an alchemy so potent that even Horace Micklethwaite's bald head was rimmed with golden fire.

She leaned back, turned her head, and speaking with the same deliberate intensity that Chanticleer had wondered at in her bearing when she first came in, began to whisper to her neighbour, a little man in glasses whose face, it seemed to Chanticleer at that moment, was stamped with every disgusting vice and depravity known to man. And yet her lips were almost brushing the lobe of his ear. She said what she had to say, and returned to her perusal of a book called *The Second World War In Pictures*. The little man took out a handkerchief and wiped his ear.

A passion surged up in Chanticleer, a passion he had not known since his mother's Pekinese, Mr Muff, had once in toddlerhood usurped his place of honour on her lap. He wanted to kill the little man in glasses, to strangle him, to tread on his face, to jump up and down again and again on his waistcoat as he lay vanquished, a sacrifice, at the feet of the adored one.

Then, oh God, and Chanticleer's knuckles whitened as he gripped the green leather and gave rein to his imperious imagination, she would seize him, drawing him to her unresisting, and lift him featherlight in her arms, pressing on his lips a kiss so terrible in its intensity that sparks would crackle in his hair and sputter at his dangling fingertips. She would stride deliberately from the Chamber, toss him masterfully down on some convenient rug, stone floor or marble bench – it mattered not to Chanticleer – and have her way with him.

He felt a hand on his shoulder, and perceived a familiar aura of brandy and cigar smoke. He turned round, and found himself looking into the blood-shot eyes, porous red nose, and obscenely gleaming lips, festooned with scraps of wet cigar tobacco, of the Minister . . .

The Mickey

Mickey Mouse, the veteran American comic, is back in London. He is here to launch the forthcoming series of his best comedies, soon to be shown here by the BBC.

Still wearing the big-buttoned Bermuda shorts, round-topped shoes and stitch-back gloves that made him famous, he greeted me in the foyer at Claridges with a sprightly grace that belied his 81 years. A simple 'Hi Pal!' a gentle wave of introduction to his wife Minnie, 79, looking charming in a mauve veil, a mauve thirties-look handbag and mauve accessories with big high-heeled shoes, and we were sunk deep in the generous sofas, sipping martinis and talking nostalgically about the Good Old Days with Pluto, Donald, Goofy and the Twins.

But the years since Hollywood's most successful husband and wife team set audiences all over the world laughing at their zany, madcap antics have not been easy, and Mickey spoke movingly of the storms that have threatened to wreck both his career and his marriage.

'You have to remember that in those days, way back in the thirties, Minnie and I were called upon to project an image of extraordinary naïvety. Fundamentally it was one of mischievous innocence, consistent with the behaviour of a normal, well-adjusted ten-year-old white Anglo-Saxon Protestant American child belonging to what you would call our successful middle class. No liquor, no violence, no sex, and above all no social comment.

'Now Minnie and I have always been deeply committed to this whole anti-war thing, whether it was against Mussolini's Germany, or Vietnam or whatever.' 'We believe war is a very terrible thing,' she agreed, nodding and fluttering her endless eyelashes with a very real sincerity, 'and we've always been against it, right from the very start.' Mickey finished his martini and ordered another round. 'But how could we convince the kids? We

116

tried introducing satirical lines into the script, I even wanted to do a whole anti-war movie where Mickey got his call-up papers and was shot up by the Japanese, just to illustrate the whole futility of it, but the Studios said they'd throw us out on our ear.' 'And we had the twins to think of,' Minnie added by way of justification, 'what could we do?'

'Then it was like I said,' Mickey lit a long cigar and brooded into the middle distance, musing on an old wound, 'there was the strain of keeping up the image off of the set. Neither Minnie nor I ever drank excessively, but the gossip writers started in on us, and boy, there wasn't a tabloid in the States didn't have some picture of one of us being thrown out of some club or other. It got so we couldn't go out in the evening.' Minnie seemed relieved to hear her husband talking so freely, and urged him to go on. 'Tell him about Pluto.'

Mickey took a long pull on his cigar, drained his martini, and turned to look me in the eye, his big ears silhouetted against the light.

'There was this story going around about me and Pluto. I know how it started, but there was nothing I could do about it, and it caused Minnie here a great deal of distress.' Minnie nods again, and almost whispers, 'Sure, I went through hell.' 'So okay. Goofy was a faggot, and he didn't care who knew it. He was made that way, I guess. So okay, he used to ask Pluto and me round to these gay clubs to keep him company when he was depressed: he'd sit there at the bar with his great big teeth hanging out and his little hat all crumpled up over one eye, and we used to just drink with him. But that's all there was to it. But not for those newspaper guys. Boy, they really had a ball.'

This was Mickey's lowest moment, and it was a cruel twist of fate that the younger generation should choose exactly that time to turn against him. 'I couldn't do a thing right. I was accused of blacking up. They used to call me Uncle Tom Mouse. They said I'd sold out and betrayed my race and class. Even the name Mickey was wrong. They said I was sneering at the Irish.' Minnie laid a hand on her husband's gently shaking shoulder and ordered another round of martinis. 'He even tried to join the Black Power people. He offered to change his name to Mustapha Ben Mouse, but they laughed in his face.'

After that every studio in the United States was closed to him.

Today, Mickey Mouse is a sad but dignified old trouper. 'We still have the twins. They're both married, for the second time, and this is for keeps, I know. We're both very happy to be in London, and we're only sorry that Donald (now Governor Duck of California) can't be here with us. I guess we should have learned from him, really: we just never understood politics.'

The Clothed Ape

A fully-grown male orang-utan that wears pale blue suits and writes 'sexy' books on a specially made jumbo-size typewriter is causing its keepers at the Konrad Lorenz Zoophysical Laboratory and Publishing House what they describe as 'acute anxiety'. After producing two copper-bottomed best-sellers in three years, there are fears that this slow-moving mountain of an ape with feathery red hair curling at the collar and cuffs of its bulging white silk shirt, spotted bow tie, huge sad sloping face, serious brown eyes and expressive white-lined black knuckles that rest so eloquently on the scarlet wall-to-wall carpet of its air-conditioned cage, may be facing a crack-up.

It is only three years ago that the twenty-stone primate, known on account of its studious appearance as 'Doctor Desmond', took the publishing world by the throat with its *Men in Fur Coats*, a sexually frank examination of the way in which the more overt and exhibitionistic mating rituals practised among monkeys can be traced to their human origins in the cocktail party and on the chaise longue. Then, last year, it leapt to the top of the publishers' charts once again, this time with its *Monkey About Town*, a searing indictment of conditions inside a modern zoo. Under the stress of an increasingly permissive regime, the orang-utan argues, many anthropoid apes are adopting more and more human behaviour patterns they observe on the other side of the bars, particularly solitary vice, mate-swapping and the formation of perverse pair-bonds.

Now, keepers fear, the big ape itself my be experiencing the agonies of self-doubt. Watching 'Doctor Desmond' as it sits slumped and sulking in the corner of its cage, shirt hanging out and suit crumpled, they have observed the slow wrinkling of the brows, the thoughtful squint, and the sudden expressions of exaggerated rage with the forearms folded on top of the head that suggest an animal who realises it is trapped. The fact that 'Doctor Desmond' has abandoned its typewriter, and therefore written nothing about its present mood, only serves to make the problem more complex, but experts believe that the orang-utan may have realised it has itself adopted a human behaviour pattern in writing sexy books, and as a result become confused and despondent.

The danger that 'Doctor Desmond' might one day make the discovery that it was subject to the same pressures and tensions as the other apes it has studied and written about with such dispassionate brilliance is one that has been uppermost in the minds of its trainers and publishers since the beginning. The climb from the bird-shrieking savagery of the Malayan jungle to the Foyle's literary lunch 'Doctor Desmond' attended after the publication of its last book is a long one, and it would be tragic if it were proved ultimately to have been in vain. To train such a hairy beast to write at all, let alone to write highly profitable and sexy books, is no mean feat, and there are many who have a very real interest in the preservation of 'Doctor Desmond's' extraordinary talent.

In its natural habitat, one trainer and publisher explained, the zoological in-group to which 'Doctor Desmond' belongs is called a 'college', and members of such a group are notoriously difficult to train. In their rude state they are treated by other orang-utans as privileged parasites or drones, provided with food and sexual partners, and allowed to survive in slothful inactivity, eating, drinking, occasionally making an indolent study of fleas, lice and other small animals that they find to hand, and spending much of their lives in mutual grooming. Apart from the 'teaching' of their young, which has been reduced in most cases to a ritual exchange of grunts and nods, they find no need to communicate, except by means of the sniggers and whoops noted during Sparrow's 'High Table' display.

Immediately after its capture 'Doctor Desmond' was encouraged to communicate its 'thoughts' by means of the typewriter, receiving a 'reward' for every page covered, however meaninglessly, and a 'shock', usually from a buff-coloured envelope pushed through the bars of the cage, for idleness. At the same time every effort was made, by dressing it in expensive shirts, ties and suits, to 'imprint' the idea that it was of a different species from the other orang-utans in captivity, who viewed it with manifest hostility, and to protect it from such influences. 'Doctor Desmond's' first lucid efforts, produced after hours of grave stabbing at the unfamiliar typewriter with a single heavy black finger, were disappointing, taking the form of an inquiry into homosexuality among sticklebacks.* Its trainers realised that there was a long way to go.

Then, three years ago, after prolonged exposure to human society, where 'Doctor Desmond' sat hunched in corners of rooms, a gin and tonic resting in its half-open palm, its eyes glazed with apparent boredom, the trainers hit the jackpot. The first references to 'pelvic thrusts', 'lobe-nibbling' and the mechanics of sexual intercourse began to appear on the type-spattered sheets torn roughly from the machine and thrust out through the bars of 'Doctor Desmond's' cage. The rewards increased, and the 'sexy' references redoubled, 'Doctor Desmond' swaying and grunting over its typewriter, teeth bared, nostrils flaring, shirt-buttons bursting off in the heat of creation.

Recently the flood of rewards had increased to such an extent that 'Doctor Desmond' had to vacate its old cage, and the unfortunate ape was forced to do battle with the horde of scavengers inevitably attracted by such a supply of good things. It is certainly not 'shocks' from the buff envelope that have brought about this strange creature's pensive melancholy. Can it be that it has heard, in the luxurious prison of the publishers' laboratory, that distant, unforgettable whooping and sniggering of the wild ones back at the 'High Table'? Something in the sad brown eyes and that huge forlorn sloping face suggests that it has.

* An interesting work on the same topic, D. Morris's 'Homosexuality in the Ten-Spined Stickleback' in *Behaviour 4*, 1952, pp. 233–61.

Making Christmas Go with a Bang

As millions foregather once again this year in the glow of the electric Yule Log and the magical glitter of the artificial candles, how many will spare a thought for a lone military figure standing bleak and windswept in the middle of Salisbury Plain, his nose red with the cold and hoary icicles showing white in his grizzled moustache? His name is Captain Mungo Wright-Charley, and as Head of the Royal Engineers Christmas Decorations and Party Novelties Testing Range at Great Borlsup he is watching over our safety at this perilously festive season as faithfully as the Good Fairy at the top of the plastic Christmas Tree.

On the grey, wet morning I visited him among the craters and charred moorland of his grim retreat, he was testing a new consignment of Happy Santa Surprise Crackers from Hong Kong. With his breath smoking white in the damp air he attached one end of the red crêpe-paper cylinder to a soot-blackened artificial 'hand' belonging to a dummy figure on a post in the uniform of a Russian infantryman. Then, after he had assured himself that the paper was held fast in the metal grip, Captain Wright-Charley painstakingly tied a length of tough twine to the other end of the cracker, and, as the seconds ticked by in tense silence, led it back to the concrete bunker where I was waiting for him. A crisp command to duck, a tug on the string, and there was a brilliant flash, followed a split second later by an earth-shaking crump. The smoke drifted away, and the charred dummy was still burning, shreds of glowing uniform floating down from the fog.

As we stalked out to find the motto, whistle and paper hat promised on the lid of the box, the Captain talked about the necessity of such tests before Christmas Decorations and Yuletide Novelties are released to the general public. 'Take a box of crackers like this, for instance: it's perfectly obvious that they could be sold without a proper sticker on the box explaining that you have to hold the whatd'yemacallit well away from the body at the moment of detonation. Otherwise there could be trouble, particularly among the elderly and the nervous. Similarly, you see, with the contents' – he found them and unrolled the motto – '*Death To The Capitalist Imperialist Jackals And The Running Dogs Of Soviet Revisionism.* Now apart from the possible damage to the eyes that could result from straining to read such small print, there is always the doom that lurks in the split pea.'

He inserted the whistle into the 'mouth' of another standing dummy, this time in the uniform of an Italian Admiral, with two rollers registering '0' showing at each of the eye-holes. 'At the back of the throat, you see, is a hypersensitive plate, which registers the probable damage to the tonsils caused by a sharply inhaled pea. Thus.' The Captain then operated a pump handle in the form of the dummy's 'arm', there was a metallic 'ping', and the figures in the eyes blurred through to 17 and 24 respectively. 'Roughly converted, that represents a thrust on impact of approximately eight hundred pounds per square inch, marginally below the acceptable limit, but all the same a nasty shock.

'Now for the paper hat test, which is infinitely more dangerous, we shall need a human volunteer. Corporal Nutbeam! Just slip off your cap comforter like a good chap and put on this blue paper Noddy Hat with appliqué imitation fur bobbles.' The Captain's voice remained crisp and matter of fact, though the ever-present danger of the situation reflected itself all too plainly in the slightly squinting eyes of Corporal Nutbeam. Gingerly, he allowed himself to be turned round and round seven times, and to be given a gentle push by the Captain in the direction of a long rising plank terminating suddenly at a height of some fifteen feet above a lightly frozen pond. As Captain Wright-Charley turned away for a moment to light his pipe and to show me the distant Indoor Testing Sheds, there was a strangled cry and a heavy splash. 'There we are, you see,' he concluded, 'oversize paper hats, slips down over your eyes during a game of Sardines, and where are you?'

Inside the Sheds other Sappers were at work with

prototype Plastigrene Christmas Trees. Shielded behind fireproof glass, they tested the first with a seated dummy, holding a twelve-inch cigar, which was made to brush past the tree in an electronically controlled wheel-chair. As the glowing tip of the cigar made contact with the tree it was immediately enveloped in a white explosion of flame, generating such an intense heat that the invalid carriage went completely out of control, careering round and round the flaming tree and propelling the dummy violently up and down in its seat. A similar effect was achieved when another tree was draped in Festifun artificial candles, and the switch was depressed from behind a glass screen by an Engineer in a steel helmet.

Walking out through laboratories full of caged guinea-pigs and supine hamsters recovering from an enforced diet of pudding-coated sixpences, dummies hanging awkwardly by the neck beside step-ladders in nooses of paperchains, and other dummies being put through simulated one-foot skids on wheeled toys and striking the floor with varying force, Captain Wright-Charley spoke modestly of his work. 'Don't worry your heads about us poor old boffins at Yuletide. We usually go somewhere nice and safe like the Germ Warfare Establishment. Happy Christmas!'

Strolling On

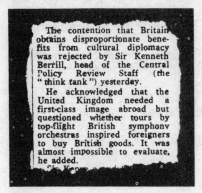

The contention that Britain
obtains disproportionate bene-
fits from cultural diplomacy
was rejected by Sir Kenneth
Berrill, head of the Central
Policy Review Staff (the
"think tank") yesterday.

He acknowledged that the
United Kingdom needed a
first-class image abroad but
questioned whether tours by
top-flight British symphony
orchestras inspired foreigners
to buy British goods. It was
almost impossible to evaluate,
he added.

Heathrow Aerodrome, January 7th. So. Out of the
gold-fish bowl at last! I have never liked the term 'think
tank', but sitting in it this morning I caught sight of my
reflection in a corroded mirror and recognised for the first
time the true cause of my aversion. In my own prominent
eyes, my mouth popping open as I puffed my pipe, I saw
not so much a Professor of Theology entering on his
sixty-sixth year as a fish in an aquarium: believing I was
communicating ideas of remarkable profundity, but to the
casual observer merely gulping air, as remote from real life
as if I inhabited another element.

Now all that has changed. I have been selected to
investigate the vexed question of whether the British
Council should continue to 'fund' cultural tours of the
European continent. The Main Chance Theatre Company,
it appears, has come to grief in Hamburg under such
auspices, while presenting a new stage version, with music,
of the *Book of Job*.

In what would seem to be an imaginative reinterpreta-
tion of the gloomy fable, Job builds an Ark, and is revealed
in the opening 'number', a hornpipe, to be, at least when

125

afloat, a passionate animal-lover, resulting in charges of gross indecency being brought by the German *Schutzpolizei*. A further mishap, according to the press cuttings, seems to have occurred in the second act, when 'a sudden cold snap' has converted the waste of waters where the dove could find no rest for the sole of her foot into a skating rink, and Job performs an ice ballet with a new character called Snow White. As ill luck would have it the British-made refrigeration plant developed some malfunction, and the orchestra stalls were suddenly flooded to a depth of one metre sixty-five, provoking a critical response from the Hamburg Press. Now I am to step in: a problem for the reductive mind to bite upon. Hoorah!

Hamburg, Hotel der Puff, January 14th. My thoughts are in a whirl. Since I arrived scarcely a wink of sleep. The whole company turned out to greet me: what wit, what unaffected joy, what incandescent, never-ending merriment! I was draped in garlands, swept up and carried shoulder high to the fleet of British Council cars outside the VIP waiting room. Parties have been given in my honour, formal dinners, champagne suppers: I am the toast of the British community.

One memorable luncheon at the British Trade Centre will serve as an example. As we trooped up the steps, Tim, our leading man, snatched a German Security Guard's peaked cap, clapped it on his head at a jaunty angle, hitched up his trousers, flung himself into the lap of a powerfully built Frau Doktor who had been reading a newspaper in the ante-room, and gave his impersonation of Marlene Dietrich.

Their leader, Joby Marmalade, leaned over as soon as we sat down, and spoke with admirable gravity – there must have been eight rather stuffy Hanseatic burghers and their ladies between us but his concentration was unwavering – of what he believes to be his sacred calling, and yet he remained watchful at every moment for anything, no matter how small, that might be lacking for my comfort. God knew, he said, that *Job* had been a disaster, but how else could we learn but by our mistakes?

Resisting the temptation to be drawn into trivialities by

the English-speaking Lady Mayoress on his right, he spoke with real understanding of other claims upon the public purse: defence, 'the boys in blue', the old folk, and above all the Third World, where the Company had enjoyed so many 'wondrous times' in desert sand or palm-fringed clearing beneath the Afric moon.

By one forty-five most of our luncheon guests were gone, but he continued among the debris of orange peel and grape-stalks to share his thoughts with me. Cradling his cigar and brandy glass in long, sensitive fingers and barely aware of Tim, who had seized up a bowl of fruit in an exquisite impromptu, and was portraying Carmen Miranda, Joby told me with tears in his eyes that he experienced moments of 'truly agonising self-examination' at the plight of 'these marvellous underdeveloped gentlemen' when he felt he couldn't touch a brass farthing of public money that 'might conceivably find its way into their poor threadbare little dhotis, bless their hearts.' Did I know what he meant?

I said I did, and recalled Our Lord's response when it was pointed out to Him that the box of spikenard used by an admirer to anoint his feet might have been sold for much money and given to the poor: 'The poor always ye have with you.' Mr Marmalade seemed to find strength in this parallel: he put down his brandy and cigar, took my head in both his hands, and kissed me on the forehead. The sudden movement unfortunately caused the stem of my pipe to become lodged at the back of my throat, but the company rallied to my assistance as a man, and the whole thing passed off as if it had been an enormous joke. And so it has gone on.

Hamburg, Hotel der Puff, January 16th. Lear opened here in Hamburg a bare four hours ago. Joby's production is unquestionably a work of genius. And yet I feel that I have been admitted to the Cave of Making, allowed to guide the potter's hand upon the wheel. Hardly a night passes but I am interrupted in my slumbers by a solid, confident knock on the door, and he strides in. He paces to and fro, tugging at his hair and beard as he speaks, and I sit up in bed, watching and listening to him spellbound. I am a natural Clown. Why have I never thought of playing the Fool? Of what use is British genius, intelligence, ideas, without a voice? Theatre *is* that voice.

Earlier this evening I heard that voice, albeit crying in the wilderness of a sparsely peopled Hamburg Schauspielhaus, and it set me aflame. Joby believes, instinctively – he never reads a play, he always 'feels it' in rehearsal – that Lear's problematic relationship with two of his daughters springs from a sado-masochistic friendship struck up late in life with Gloucester, and Tim does it all in black leather and stainless steel chains.

One English member of the audience left after five minutes, denouncing it as 'mindless drivel', but Joby was magnificent. He gripped my knee in the darkness, his face in the glow from the stage a study in injured resignation. I reminded him in a whisper that a prophet is not without honour save in his own country. Moments later, one of Tim's punishment wristlets snapped while Gloucester was making him lick candyfloss from between the spokes of his motorbike; both the Germans present got up and left with heavy Teutonic jeers at the expense of the British Steel Corporation, and Joby never so much as flinched. I am writing my report tonight.

134, Sabena Gardens SW7, January 20th. I do not understand the tone of the chairman's announcement to the Press, still less his curtly worded postcard. Let him do his worst. I cannot wait to see Joby's face when he holds auditions for the Canadian tour of *Lear*.

Room at the Top

Seven men on Everest summit

Three Frenchmen and an Austrian have reached the summit of Mount Everest, close on the heels of the three West Germans from the same expedition who scaled the 29,000ft. peak on Saturday night. The leader of the French group was a former minister   **Page 6**

With its breathtaking views, highly exclusive clientele and pristine loveliness, 'Evercrest' has for many seasons now enjoyed world-wide renown as a beauty-spot where top people can put their feet and much else up in uniquely nice surroundings.

Today, with growing affluence and a sense of adventure bringing dream holidays within the reach of those for whom, a generation ago, they might have seemed about as likely as going to the moon, 'Evercrest' is able to extend the same out-of-this-world welcome to a chosen few more.

It is often the case that a broadening of the scope *vis à vis* the clientele has meant a subsequent collapse of standards, and everything going downhill. We at 'Evercrest' are determined that this shall not be the case *chez nous*.

We would therefore request, while extending the heartiest welcome to you to come and 'take a peek through the roof of the world' as Robert Louis Stevenson put it, that as an 'Evercrest' Camper you will kindly abide by the few but necessary rules which it has seemed reasonable for us to insist upon.

1.   Kindly leave the summit of Mount Everest as you would wish to find it. It is not just there for you. Many others will be waiting to use it immediately after you and their feelings must be respected.

2.   No washing of any kind, rinsing through woollens, soaking smalls or boiling of soiled linen, is to be done on the Peak. This is not what it is there for. Adequate washing facilities are available at the various Camp Sites (Cold Water only, Tuesdays 7.30 to 8.30), and the Snow White Hand Laundry (on flat rocks above Second Cataract, ask for Mrs Thumper) collects on Fridays in rotation. It is also expressly forbidden to use the Summit Area for drying, with or without clothes-lines. Many complaints have been received from Campers taken aback at finding intimate items hanging on the sharp bit at the top and following discussions it has been decided that all activities involving personal laundry must cease forthwith.

3.   It is forbidden to use transistor radios or gramophones in the area of the Peak after dusk. A selection of popular medleys will be played as per normal during the hours of darkness through the loudspeakers situated on the tall poles at the Camp Perimeters and those guilty of spoiling the quiet enjoyment of others by playing loud Classical Music etc. will be subject to on-the-spot fines and the confiscation of personal radios. Living together under the somewhat cramped conditions imposed by the Camping Area can create unpleasant friction (see the paragraphs below relating to First Aid, Fire and Ambulance Services, Riot Control etc.) and if forbearance is not exercised on a voluntary basis then it will be enforced.

4.   Children and dogs are only allowed on the lower slopes under the strictest supervision, and in the Summit Area they must be kept on a lead at all times. This precaution is dictated only by common sense. Both toddlers and pets can easily become lost in dense crowds, particularly when physical movement for adults is very restricted, and the responsibilities of 'Evercrest' Leisure Services Ltd (Nassau) do not extend to combing the surrounding valleys for runaways.

5.   Campers are required to take all litter away with them. The dropping of lolly sticks, plastic cups, extruded polystyrene picnic packs, vandalised hot drink dispensers, sections of metal fencing etc., down the Western Cwm, a purpose for which it was not intended, has in the past led to many unpleasant fatalities among those wating below, and can cause serious blockages to an already very overloaded system.

6.   Campers are asked kindly to refrain from plugging electric razors, vibrators, hair-dryers etc. into the fairy-light circuit at the top of the mountain. Mr Tensing's father is not by any means as young as he was, and as Chief Technical Operative in charge of Electrical Maintenance it is not right that he should be got out of bed several times a night, as was often the case until recently, to walk all the way up to the summit in order to replace a fuse.

7.   'Queueing' is a feature of life generally accepted with a wry grin by seasoned campers, but discipline is vital if any progress at all is to be maintained towards the Summit. All busking, whether it be in the form of tap-dancing, singing to guitar accompaniment, or extempore public speaking directed against the management, is expressly forbidden, and is punishable in extreme cases with summary execution. Panic is an ugly spectacle at the best of times, and among tightly packed crowds on an icy and in some cases sharply sloping surface it can be very disagreeable indeed. Parties are required to wear uniform jerkins in the colour of their Camp, which facilitates the marshalling of queues, always a slow business and one requiring a high measure of cooperation from Campers, especially in sub-zero temperatures. These jerkins will be found to have a number on the front, to prevent 'queue-barging', and a circular target motif on the back to assist in crowd control.

8.   Emergencies arise in the best-regulated Camps: hysteria has been known to break out in the queues, and there have been regrettable instances of Campers attempting to make their escape by tobogganing over the heads of fellow-Campers on tin trays, disguising themselves in fur coats and announcing themselves to be Abominable

Snowmen, or merely attacking one of the Marshals. Should such an emergency arise, Campers should inform the nearest Marshal if he is not already aware of it, and he will sound the alarm – a high whooping siren – which will alert the Civilian Emergency Services. Campers will then be sprayed by helicopter for their own protection with a paralysing gas until the emergency is over.

And now, enjoy the holiday of a lifetime!

Into the Stocks

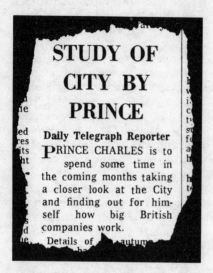

STUDY OF CITY BY PRINCE

Daily Telegraph Reporter

PRINCE CHARLES is to spend some time in the coming months taking a closer look at the City and finding out for himself how big British companies work.

Details of autumn

The mood is one of hushed expectancy. In the lofty, golden gloom of this ancient, stone-vaulted Moneylenders' Hall, where for centuries the great cut-throats and robber-barons of the Old World have gathered amid the trumpets and the pageantry to carve out the bloody history of Europe, an army of cleaners, florists, caterers, costumiers and decorators has been at work since dawn to set the scene for this especial day.

And an especial day this most assuredly is. Because today Prince Charles Edward Oliver Smettigrew Montmorency Gules Birtwistle Rin Tin Tin Horace Nelly Sinatra de los Angeles Mutt y Jefe, Duke of Cornwall, by the Grace of God High Privy Keeper and Prince of the Welsh, is to re-forge the massy links that bind the Monarch to his City, to illumine with the solemn majesty of ritual those underpinnings of the Throne that the Victorian,

133

Edwardian and Georgian ages thought it more prudent to conceal from the vulgar.

Ever since the Prince's great forebear, Henry the Eighth, swept the spiritual power of the Church into his broad embrace, it has been considered seemly for Members of the Ruling House, however advanced and enlightened their view of private morals, to be seen hobnobbing with Bishops and Archbishops on terms of easy jocularity.

Traditional ties with the armed services, too, have been maintained. It might be considered undignified in some circles, were the Queen to be photographed detonating a nuclear device or taking too close an interest in the manufacture of nerve gas, but that has not prevented military uniform, from the archaic to the relatively modern, and tricked out with the insignia of physical gallantry on the field of battle, from becoming a familiar part of any monarch's official wardrobe.

Of the real power, however, in whose defence all the intricate hierarchies of the Army, Navy and Air Force have evolved in that golden tapestry of death and destruction that is the history of these islands, the Royal Family has in recent times fought shy.

It was even thought that the carrying of money about the Royal Person might in some way sully the pure lustre of royalty.

But now, today, when in a few seconds the great doors of the Moneylenders' Hall are thrown open and three herald trumpeters play a fanfare of welcome with Cash Register accompaniment, Prince Charles will give official recognition to his own long-unacknowledged realm. He will be in it, as one observer termed it, up to the neck.

A last-minute flurry of activity as the official decorators adjust the floral garlands concealing the sawn-off shotguns and machine carbines carried by the Most Worshipful Order of Merchant Bankers, a few shiny faces are powdered by make-up men skilled in the art of 'taking down' razor scars and filling in the line of a nicked ear, air-freshener is sprayed once again over the gleaming heads of the waiting dignitaries, and all is ready.

First, the great coded knock, traditionally used by

bankers with 'hot money' to dispose of: three bangs, a bell, fourteen more bangs in quick succession, a multiple rattle of the lock, and then the high doors burst open to a violent kick from the boot of Lord Capone, Most Honourable Keeper of the Takings. A colourful figure, a cigar smouldering in the corner of his mouth, wearing the traditional crumpled suit and bearing in his arms the tommy-gun of office.

Behind him now, the Prince, looking strangely innocent in such company, and dressed in the uniform of a Gentleman Employee of the City: black shoes gleaming, striped trousers, black jacket, rolled umbrella, and a bowler hat. Following him, the Bulls and Bears of the Rough Mob, the elite servants of the City, poised at a moment's notice to fly to any corner of the globe to intervene on behalf of British Business Interests.

Lord Capone leads the Prince in stately progress between the ranks of formally-robed Asset-Strippers and Currency Speculators, there are handshakes, heads nod in greeting, and a murmur of introduction to each. Then questions, and Lord Capone explains the golden death's-head decorations worn by those whose initiatives have resulted in particularly high unemployment, despair or suicide in those companies they have taken into their care.

Now the Prince is being led towards the podium, where the American Emissaries, together with representatives of the Central Intelligence Agency and the Mafia Corporation Worldwide, wait to make the formal presentation of the Prince Bernhardt of the Netherlands Award.

There is suddenly some confusion at the other end of the Hall. The great doors had been closed again but there seems now to be considerable pressure being brought to bear on them from outside. Indeed, one of the upper panels has just splintered to admit what looks like the barrel of a medium-sized field gun.

This would seem to be unscheduled: there is no mention of it in the official programme, and from immediate reaction inside the hall the disturbance does not seem entirely welcome.

Another splintering crash, now, and the great doors fall majestically inwards to reveal that the gun barrel is in fact

135

mounted on a tank: standing in the armoured turret the dignified and familiar city figure, Sir Baby-face 'One-leg' Dacosta, Lord Capone's great rival in the field of British finance.

A thrilling moment of pageant and ceremonial, and it's anyone's guess what will happen next.

(*The remainder of the transcript is at present being pieced together at the Home Office Micro-Archaeological Research Department, Coney Hatch.*)

On Ilkley Moor b'aht Frog

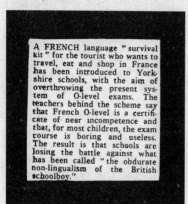

A FRENCH language "survival kit" for the tourist who wants to travel, eat and shop in France has been introduced to Yorkshire schools, with the aim of overthrowing the present system of O-level exams. The teachers behind the scheme say that French O-level is a certificate of near incompetence and that, for most children, the exam course is boring and useless. The result is that schools are losing the battle against what has been called "the obdurate non-lingualism of the British schoolboy."

Right, lads, let's be havin yer. Tek yer boots off desk, Scragley, pin yer lugholes back an yer might learn summat. Headmaster, Mr Postlethwaite, is in a right lather, and I fully understand his apoplexy, about standard of performance in French O Levels. They were bloody diabolical. Half of you seemed to be under impression Voltaire were a type of ventilation plant used in factories to keep temperature down, and Mr Postlethwaite tells me that when he mentioned Racine results he distinctly saw three members of this class pull out bettin slips. They may not, either of em, have had the advantage of bein born British, but they were both great Soccer players in their day and deserve to be remembered.

I personally attribute abysmal showing, though I wouldn't say it outside this classroom, to fact that teachin of French in this school has bin left in the twitchy and tremblin hands of Monsewer so-called Morris, a right shag in my opinion, with filthy personal habits, who might well learn a bit about gettin pickled onions an garlic off his breath before he starts teachin decent Yorkshire lads about how to talk foreign.

As your PT Instructor it has fallen to me to tell you that we have now changed all that. Monsewer Morris as I understand it is at this moment having his bones shaken to the marrow on hovercraft, on route, as they say down there, for eight weeks compulsory vacation in his country of origin, and we shall in future be equippin you with a brand new Survival Kit enablin any ordinary sensible lad with a tongue in his head to remain alive for up to seven days, assumin he has necessary protective clothin, water-purifying tablets an lurgi pills, even in an utter muckhole like Paris.

First off then, an I'll have that catapult if you please, Codrington, is to realise that Frog as a lingo is on its last legs. A dinosaur, waiting only for a sufficiently hard poke in ribs to crumble to dust. Quite apart from havin no satisfactory equivalent for such scientific terms as rog-wobble, scrintin baffle readjuster or Pontefract cake, Frog is hamstrung with countless archaic forms that effectively prevented it from ever draggin itself gruntin and gesticula-tin out of twelfth century, let alone Middle Ages. *Lee* and *Lah*, to tek but one glarin example. Any form of communication that designates a hobnailed boot, *Lah Bott*, as feminine, or a brassiere, *Lee Soo-cha Gawj*, as masculine has clearly got its evolutionary knickers in a twist with disastrous results.

History has also bin against it. Had things turned out different history-wise, *Lah Bott* would no doubt be upon other foot, but as it is your speaker of Frog has got his back against wall and is lookin dead worried. Pockets of resistance there may be, notably among political extrem-ists in Quebec, driven mad no doubt by havin to talk to other Canadians for a couple of hundred years, bits of Africa an odd desert islands dotted about where they still jabber a variety of Frog, albeit incomprehensible to man or beast on account of dinner plates stuck in their lips, but in point of fact what were once reckoned language of diplomacy is now entirely up spout.

Certainly Mainland Frog has taken a right poundin, what with pop records, telly an Scotch Soccer Hooligans swarmin all over em smashin place up, with result your ordinary Frog in Street has had to pull himself together an learn English like everybody else, if only for his own protection. The fact that those with a financial interest in keepin em prattlin away in Frog – book writers, makers of spare parts with instructions on in Frog they can't flog off to anyone else etcetera – have had laws passed sayin anyone as gets nabbed usin English words can be strung up by thumbs or for persistent offences burned at stake, only indicates cracks as are appearin in this whole superannuated edifice. It is through these cracks, lads, you will be well advised to direct the spearhead of your attack.

Examinin the form in front of you entitled *University of York Survival Kit*, and stop doin that Arkenshaw or you will have even greater difficulty in decipherin small print, you will see:

Exercise One: 'Askin Way and Understanding Directions.' Askin is one thing, understandin is another. However the followin basic plan should serve.
SURVIVAL SQUADDY: Eiffel Tower.
ALIEN: Jabber jabber jabber, waves arms about, rolls eyes etc.
SS: EI-FFEL TOW-ER.
A: Jabber jabber, points.
SS: Right, why didn't you bloody say so in the first place.

Exercise Two: 'Shoppin for Food, Souvenirs, Post Cards, Stamps Etc.' This has been made easier by almost complete penetration of Frog market by Yank brand-names but SS will be required to show some familiarity with Frog manners an a lynx-eyed interest in cash register at end of transaction.
SS: *See-voo Play*. I would like a Jumbo Packet of Frosticles, a bottle of milk, Mannekin Pis bottle opener, one Greetings from Paris with two ladies twangin each others' knicker elastic, and one o' them. Licks thumb and presses down on corner of postcard.
A: Jabber jabber.
SS: An I'll have that writ out in figures unless you're lookin for a knuckle sandwich.

Exercise Three: 'Go to a Caff or Restaurant.' No problem. They are all called Self-Service or Drugstore and

139

Frog has largely bin eliminated from vocabulary. However to avoid bein stung, observin *Bong-shaw* on enterin will ensure you are taken for a local.

Exercise Four: 'Travel by Rail or Road.' Motorin, the Frog expression *Murd*, pronounced on windin down the car window, may be of some assistance. Goin by train, remember that unlike England many place names in France do not sound the same as they look. E.g.

SS: Rheims. There an back.

A: Speaking indistinctly through little amplifier in hatch, Jabber jabber.

SS: Rheims Froggichops an stop muckin about I've got a train to catch.

A: Jabber jabber jabber. Hangs label over little hatch saying *Ferm*.

SS: Sod that for a lark. Moves label sayin *Ferm*, reaches through little hatch, takes felt-tip pen an writes Rheims on ticket desk. There, pointing to place name, an Back, pointing to station entrance.

A: Produces ticket.

SS: *Mur-see*.

Exercise Five: 'Stay in a Hotel, Youth Hostel, Campsite or a French Home.' Trick question, this. Correct answer is, unless you're after terminal diarrhoea, fleas the size of a man-eating crab or a nasty dose of t'other, *don't*. Keep movin, sleep when you get back to Wetherby. Frog thieves have been known to strip sleepin visitors down to skellintons.

Summin up, you're goin into battle, lads. In recent years, your Frog has forced us to scrap half-crown, bob and tanner, threatened to wipe out pounds an ounces, and now has effrontery to try an massacre your inches feet yards an miles, 'for convenience of visitors from abroad'. A hysterical, last ditch counter-attack, comparable to Battle of Bulge, noted Ardennes Offensive, when Krauts also knew in their heart of hearts that they were done for. Frog, as a language, make no mistake about it, will soon collapse entirely, 'for the convenience of visitors from abroad'. You, lads, will be forefront of that assault. God bless you all, and in with *Lah Bott*.

Big Game

It was only a few weeks ago that the Duke of Edinburgh suggested re-vigorating the wild life of Scotland by stocking certain areas with wild boar. Now, it seems, the wild boar at least have taken his advice. Breaking out of their relative captivity on a private estate in the Lowlands, they are reported to be multiplying fast and striking terror into the kilted inhabitants.

One person to whom the story will come as no surprise is Lord Sponge, the witty hereditary peer and entertainment magnate. Single-handed he has turned Grislies, his ancestral home set in four acres of fun-fairs and discarded ice-cream wrappers just off the B7231 somewhere to the north of Scrim, into a unique institution. After several early setbacks in the realm of local nudist stalking and home-made bomb manufacture, he went into wild animals in a big way in 1967, losing an arm and a leg. Since then the visitors have come in their tens of thousands to feed his swiftly increasing herds of blue rhino, mastodon, pygmy gorilla and sabre-toothed land crabs. They are still hungry.

Then came the news that many species had been climbing over the electrified fences and secretly breeding in the three-and-sixpennies at Scrim's recently redecorated Ritz Essoldo. Rumours ran rife, as did the patrons of the Ritz Essoldo. Newspapermen from all over the world tramped warily through the narrow streets, and the night was turned into day as Scrim's dignitaries sat under dazzling television lights, cautiously answering the probing inquiries of Japanese and Zambian interviewers. All that was uncovered in the way of 'hard' evidence was a set of huge footprints, and three unconfirmed sightings of a Yeti-like creature in an ankle-length fur coat leaning against walls with one hand and belching.

Nevertheless, international interest in Lord Sponge's rampaging carnivores has come as a much needed shot in the arm to Scrim's hitherto quiet tourist trade. The town's major and only hotel, the Gleneagles Guest House, has built on a nissen-hut style extension, attractively roofed in two-tone bri-thatchlon; and car mascot monsters in green rubber, postcards showing a King Kong type monkey cleaning its fingernails with the spire of Scrim Church, snow-storm paperweights and comic ashtrays sell like hot cakes both in Scrim itself and outside the wrought iron and neon gates of Grislies. This boom, locals are the first to admit, has done much to temper their dismay at the break-outs.

Lord Sponge himself is a noisy, advancing man with steel teeth and a fierce glitter in his eye. Known locally as the Moshe Dayan of Scrim, he conducts his fund-raising campaigns with dignity and stealth, and is satisfied that wild animals have put the roof back on Grislies several times over. Certainly it looks like it. He likes to think, all the same, that he is 'emotionally involved' with his animals, and despite one unfortunate experience when he was punched on the nose by a jealous male baboon, it is a policy he intends to push through come what may. His dreams of fostering periodical escapes and the un-trammelled breeding of exotic animals in urban areas is essentially a disinterested one and wholly untainted with commercial considerations.

'There's been a lot of nonsense in the press about my work for the Sponge Night Life Fund,' he told me as we sipped tranquillisers in the observation chamber above the Pit, where visitors can try their strength against a 'surprise pack' of wild animals and no questions asked, 'suggestions that I blow it all on taking attractive female gorillas to the South of France, dancing with wildebeestes in expensive night clubs, that sort of thing. Of course there is that side, I'd be the last to make any bones about it, but ultimately what I am about in permitting these big fellows out is a total restoration of man's natural environment. You've heard the word. That's what I'm up to.'

In theory, Lord Sponge's plan sounds both plausible and attractive. Man, he claims, has become increasingly alienated from his natural surroundings. With more and more zoos and safari parks adopting the 'open cage' principle the atmosphere of natural jungle terror will once again be achieved, with gorillas suddenly emerging from underground public lavatories, lions lurking in the lift, and poisonous creatures infesting Government offices. Whether, in practice, the Government will find the competition too keen remains to be seen.

Who But Schubert?

The Offshore Rubbishdump

As a thinking Hamburger, I have been for a lifetime soaked in the old Hanseatic Port. But I am, at the deepest bottom, a Euroburger.

Before being immersed in the cream of European High Society in the thirties, I found myself for a brief but emotionally intense interlude rubbing shoulders with the Wet Bobs of a Well-known English Boys' Public School. Linguistically, of course, this meant being thrown in at the Deep End, over and over again. But with such success that I am still frequently quizzed, at Uppermiddleclass dinner parties, both in London and Macclesfield (where we have a little country place) by would-be Professors Higgins, wanting to know exactly where I learned to speak so perfect an old Queen's English.

Here now, both in my capacity as a roving Euro-Councillor and as Head of the mighty Hans Niesenbumsidäsi AG of Hamburg-Harburg, I like to feel that while holding myself for cultural reasons somewhat aloof above the sluggish and stagnant mainstream of British life, I nevertheless have one foot always in it.

I would like therefore, in all humility, as dear Frank Longford would say, to proffer my observations. How does old Britannia look from where I am sitting on the Board of our British Subsidiary, Union Jack Royal Empire Holdings of Windsor Ltd?

To some of my fellow-countrymen, who grew up perhaps among the Ruins that Tommy Knocked About a Bit, the image of Britain is not always 100 per cent positive. A kind of Offshore Rubbishdump, perhaps, inhabited by sometimes savage, always feckless natives under the influence of the United States and expensive alcohol, ludicrously incapable of governing themselves and yet oddly resistant to any overt assumption of the reins of office either by the Japanese or West German firms who provide the economic infrastructure.

'Fine, OK,' even these harsh critics will admit with an indulgent chuckle of mirth, 'let them by all means keep all their old tribal customs: their Master of Rolls, the meaningless ritual of their Stately Opening of the Parliament, of their Picket Lines, their economic black magic and other mumbo-jumbo. After all, hundreds of thousands of West German Tourists have annually to expose millions of metres of West German Filmstock to something: why not to Johann Bull's colourful and romantic old doings?'

But with developments *vis à vis* the United States, on what under Mr Reagan's interregnum might be called the Western Front, I find them less in sympathy.

Piccadilly's Trocadero Site, I learned at a *soirée* in Pimlico on Thursday night, is to be redeveloped as a publicly acknowledged Base for American Activities. Humiliated by a mighty replica Saturn Rocket, the manhood of Britain will be taken for a ride of the type pioneered by the American arch-Nationalist Wilf Disney.

Following the rigid and doctrinaire lines laid down by British neo-Disneyites, Britain's youth will be subjected, I am told, to 'experiences', ostensibly perhaps of a British-European nature. In fact, yet another subtle means of further intensifying the cultural omnipresence of the American Occupation.

To the man on top of the Lüneburg Omnibus, this is of course as plain as a pancake. From a pan-European point of view, too, it seems somewhat disloyal, not to say ungrateful. Particularly when a German firm, then under the direction of Hermann Goering, put in such a splendid effort, even working nights, to clear the site.

Gang Ho!

Hoorah for the Democratic Socialites! These at least were the feelings that bubbled up under my shirtfront on Wednesday night as I sauntered in my smoking tuxedo into the candlelit glories of St Solomon's College, Oxford, for a fund-raising Beano.

By the time I left, when rosy-fingered Morning was already sitting on one dreaming spire after another, it was Hoorah no longer. It was Thrice Hoorah, Glory Be and Hallelujah! My God, what a Party!

The Master, my close friend Dr the Hon. Cedric de Vere Pratt-Fortescue-Birtwhistle, DD, had reacted strongly to the petrol in the Budget and had forthwith thrown up his lot with the Four Gangsters. Simple running costs, he explained to me over a brimming silver tankard of Amontillado in the Combinations Room, would rocket through the ceiling. Even picking up the bill for three helicopters to blow-dry his private croquet lawn the day before he had been knocked pie-eyed with amazement.

For a lifelong, true-blue, dyed-in-the-woollens Tory, following Mr Christopher Stickleback-Fowler across the floor had been no easy task, but he had done it with his teeth clenched, hanging on to Mrs Shelley Winters's undertakings.

I was not, I discovered somewhat to my surprise and to my beloved wife Hildegard's manifest displeasure, as we took our places in the Hall, Guest of Honour. This prime slot was occupied by a fat, quite affable chap with specs, who told me after a certain amount of probing and the request that he should speak more clearly, that his name was Boy Jenkins.

'No relation of the would-be Head Gangster?' I quipped, and indulged over the caviar in a little pawky fun at the expense of that Galloping Gastronome who, I gathered, during his tenure of high European office, had personally demolished many a mountain of *pâté de foie gras* and drained many a wine-lake single-handed. Only as he gave me a fishy look and lowered his lips into the claret did it strike me with the force of a hard blow between the ears: what a gaffe!

St Solomon's, I became aware as quaintly costumed menials bore in an immense hunch of Venison, and more varieties of fine wine gurgled into the sparkling array of glasses at my elbow, has not perhaps felt the snip of Mrs Thatcher's educational secateurs as keenly as some other institutions. Nevertheless, practical economics always having been my strong bow, and bearing in mind the logistics that will be entailed in getting the Democratic Socialite Aeroplane off the ground, I felt it recumbent upon me to take out my pocket calculator and get weaving on some figures.

'How much did the Master think this caviar had cost us *per capitum*? How much was the porous-nosed old buttling fellow being paid in overtime? What exactly was the identity of the "Entrepreneur" who happened to have run over the venison? What was the rough value "under the hammer" of the immense silver-gilt bowl filled with rosewater in which the old Fellows were washing their necks after the eleventh course? Was any extra fee being paid to the picturesquely attired choristers who materialised on the menstruals' gallery at some moment, now hazy in my mind, in order to sing an eight-part unaccompanied Latin Cantata?'

These and other tough-nosed questions of *Realpolitik* I put to my new Democratic Socialite comrades. Their answers flew fast and thick over the groaning-board. *In vino veritas!* Some argued that costly blow-outs were a good wheeze to raise a bit of Wind from the Right. Others said, on the contrary, it was their true friends of the Left who really appreciated the *haute cuisine*, and that no back-to-back ex-artisan's dwelling in Limehouse (as they could well vouch) was without its new edition of the *Good Food Guide*. *Crème brûlé*, supermarket custard and cold porridge were all lobbed hugger-mugger into the debate, falling on far from deaf ears.

At the height of this exhilarating political ding-dong,

however, the true Piggie-in-the-Middle spirit of Centrism re-asserted itself. A Truce was called, we withdrew to cleanse our palates with Perrier Water, I was urged not to rock the boat until we had a ha'porth of tar, and we returned to attack the Dessert, Nuts, Cheese and 67 varieties of Liqueur in a new mood of unity.

What an inspiration these Democratic Socialites are! Their statesmanlike cries of 'Moderation!' 'Oh, I say, come on!' and 'What an agreeable piece of Brie!' ring in my ears even now.

Out with the Barclaycards and Excess, I say. Fasten your safety belts, brothers, if they will still do up, and stand by for rip-off!

The Tiddling Pond

Often, as I listen to the big early-nineteenth century hit tunes composed by my great-great-great uncle Franz Schubert, I find myself regretting that he did not follow the other branch of the family into Heavy Engineering. With that kind of money behind him, what a diplomat he would have made!

Such thoughts floated across my mind on Friday night at a Charity Concert given in Billingsgate Fishmarket by the Dowager Queen Mother-in-Law to be, Dame Barbaria Cartland. As Monty Sunshine and his Syncopated Foot-warmers hit us with the 'Trout' the whole audience – tiaras, white ties, lapdogs and other miniaturised decorations – was submerged under a warm flood of *je ne sais quoi* and everyone was carried away. But fish still hung in the air.

As one who has known Helmut Schmidt since he went in his leather knickers, I had been jumped on by all and sundry before the Concert. Who did he think he was? Why had he tried to get up Mrs Thatcher's nose? Wasn't all this Euro-fishy-business a bit of a red herring in the woodpile?

Now the 'Trout' was well and truly off, I decided to open the whole can of beans for the benefit of my hostess, on whose right hand I had the pleasure of being seated. 'Are not fish after all,' I postulated for a kick-off, 'deeply symbolic of our relationship one with the other in the Big Pond that is Europe?'

My gracious companion inclined her head, offering me a lovely pearly-bright smile amid the frou-frou of white fur and the darkly-passionate undertow of the Music, splashing like great sea-waves from the walls of the Fishmarket. I took the plunge.

Here we have, I mused, the Big Fish, Little Fish, Sprats and Toddlers all mooching about before the creation of Europe . . . Rock Salmon, Haddocks, Plaices, Flounders, Guitarfishes, Dolly Varden Trouts, Horse Mackerels,

Barn Door Skates, Butterfishes, Sharks, Bass, Anchovies, Stingrays and Flying Gurnards and so on without being too precise. My hostess nodded. Free fish, strangers as it were to saddle and bridle. From time to time, amateur efforts are made to catch them. On the inland waterways – and here I noticed my companion make a minute adjustment to her hearing device – idle old codgers sit dangling their apparatus in the water waiting for a bite. Ditto on the Ocean Wave.

Will they, I asked rhetorically, and bearing in mind the Brotherhood-of-Europe, run into a French *matelot* who will, with a cruel twist of his moustaches, stun them with a violent electric shock? An old British seadog who will blow them out of the water with High Explosive? A lugubrious Hollander who will lure them into his Polder and strangle them?

Even if our fish has the good fortune to swim into the ken of a decent German Fisherman, the stiff breezes rustling in his silvery sideboards as he draws in the nets through weather-battered old hands, the mesh, before Euro-standards were imposed, might be too big: years more of tedium swimming about.

Eventually, of course, when Europe is a reality, and everything else, like the State under Socialism, has withered away and dropped off, there will be no more of that. Fish too will be standardised and metricated, bred in chunky, pre-filleted, easy-to-stack shapes, their entire life-cycle contained in the shallow bubbling water of a high-density fishfarm, freed for ever from Angst.

The Baritone Arthur Mullard swept us along with Goethe's unforgettable ditty 'The Fisherman':

> '. . . and out of the foaming waters
> A soaking-wet lady bursts . . .'

My Hostess turned to me with a look almost of possession in her radiant eyes. I was not the cold fish she had always thought. Had I given her the plot of a new Romantic Novella?

Iron in the Cox

Being the involuntary subject of a bungled assassination bid is certainly no picnic. One's wither was inevitably wrung on Monday evening by the painful spectacle of the faded matinée idol and Ruler of the Western World, though certainly no chicken, being trussed up and bundled into his limousine the moment the hot lead started to whistle.

How different from our own Graf Bismarck when he encountered the same irritating contretemps. Shot through the recto at pot-blank range, he spun about in a trice, gripped the incompetent by one wrist, and held him dangling until the Berlin Boys in Blue were able to thunder up the *trottoir* and enlist his help with their inquiries. Bismarck was of course a German, and beside the Iron Chancellor any contemporary like Sir Geoffrey Howe must inevitably look like something the cat has to some extent had for breakfast.

Nevertheless, the old Blood and Iron Merchant's illustrious name was very much upon our lips yesterday afternoon, when I joined my close friend Dr the Hon. Cedric de Vere Pratt-Fortescue-Birtwhistle DD, Master of St Solomon's College, Oxford, and his companion Mr Edward Heath in the Oxford Launch for the Boat Race.

The old Count had given his name to one of our greatest feats of German nautical engineering, I recalled. Your chaps had sunk it, OK. This kind of thing happens when the healthy spirit of European competitiveness for overseas markets becomes a little overheated; no use crying about spilt milk.

The Oxford boat jerked away in front of us, being propelled through the choppy water by burly oarsmen, one of them under the direction of the female of the species.

I think it is no secret that the erstwhile Premier and

world-class *matelot* Mr Heath has always been fairly fond of his scoff, and is now wrestling – tactfully ignored by a discreet and sympathetic Press as always sensitive to the canons of good taste – with a touch of hyper-inflation on the weight front. Supplied however with a four-kilo bag of low-cal chocolate biscuits to keep him going until teatime, our Eurohero was on sparkling form.

In his own dizzy days of power, we would linger over the cigars and *petit fours*, seedcake, *Prinzregententorte*, old scraps of French bread, cold potatoes and savoury taramasalata dips left behind after great dinners in the Chancelleries of Europe, often until breakfast time. On one such occasion I had reminded him of Goethe's famous image of the State in *Faust*, *Part II*, that of an Elephant.

Now, as we churned our way through the bobbing flotsam of rotting timber, plastic washingupliquid containers, dead pigeons and so forth between Putney and Mortlake, I asked him, wiping the spray from my spectacles as he peered through narrowed eyes at the prow, whether he had ever considered the Oxford Boat was in some ways a more appropriate Simulacrum of the British State? Eight brawny chaps going in the wrong direction – what better image of the Cabinet? – steered with consummate skill and verve by their sexual inspiration, going in the Right direction (I paused to underline this quite amusing pun), the little woman.

'What little woman?' the bronzed survivor of Fastnet but not of Tory wrath enquired, his jowls tightening for a scrap. When I unsheathed the person of whom I was thinking as the incomparable Margaret Hilda, I was engulfed in a veritable roaring Niagara of information about the Iron Cox, much of which to my surprise the Editor of this liberal, no-holds-barred investigative journal absolutely refuses to print.

Such indeed was the vehemence of the bouffant-haired ex-Leader that the Race was long over, Cedric Birtwhistle's other guests long since departed, when he finally ingested the last shreds of the paper bag that had contained the chocolate biscuits and concluded his thumbnail sketch of the politician he persisted in referring to, like the heroine of Haggard Rider's novel, as 'She'.

Mr Benn, it would appear, is not the only one with sufficient oomph, given a fair wind, to split his party allegiances.

Adolf, Winnie and the Pledge

History, like the Senior Partner of the Holy Trinity, moves in a highly mysterious way. Now forwards, now sideways, now backwards, now by a series of amazing lopes and bends, now, as in your traditional Morris Oxford Folkdance the Hokey Cokey, 'jumping up and down like this, Oy.'

This revelation struck me with all the force of a well-oiled boxing-glove filled with scrap-metal on Monday last in Liverpool at a Nuremberg-style rally of massed alcoholics. We were being addressed by the tiny, piping, ex-drinker Screaming Lord Avebury, better known from his days of Liberal indulgence as the fun-loving Member hanging out at Orpington, Eerie Pillock.

During the early forties, when the present dominant Franco-German alliance was being forged in the white-hot cut and thrust of debate that was the Blitzkrieg, I was encouraged to believe that your own Führer, Sir Winston, was a tope, a soaker, so paralytically drunk as to have to support himself on his cigar when going round corners, hurling down highly explosive bombs on our innocent cattle and poultry in rural areas. Hitler, on the other hand, was seen as a bit of a sobersides who liked a Perrier Water with ice and lemon.

Come the sharp downturn in the German economy in 1945, I am asked to revise this somewhat simplistic black-and-white image in the light of a loaded field-gun pointed at my head by our American and British visitors. Churchill, in a shake of a lamb's tail, metamorphosises into a merry, cherry-nosed old codger, always ready with two fingers for the proletariat; a man who might from time to time accept a half shandy but never when he was operating the heavy machinery of international power.

Hitler by contrast had been a drug-addict, so desperate for a drink at all hours of the day and night as to suck it through the cracks of a tightly sealed beer-barrel until he frothed at the mouth.

Thirty-five years fly by, with all their kaleidoscope-fragmentary woof and weft of sexual misunderstandings, restaurant meals, diplomatic how-is-your-father, and my wife Hildegard's continuing cystitis. And now here I was, sitting cheek by cheek with the flower of British Dipso-mania, in this bubbling *entrepôt* once infested by the Beatles, being told by a Peer of the Realm that Churchill was after all a tope, a soaker, etc., just as our PR Chappie, Jo Goebbels, had always told us. Then some Sir Charlie popped up to geld his Lily by announcing that Hitler was of course a toeteetaller. You could, as I say, have knocked me down with a grand piano.

The meeting over, I got hold of the Noble Lord by the button holes. I was in no mood to beat about his bush. Casting myself in the role of the Doubting Tom-Cat I challenged him to show me proof of his scandalous tale: all-night binges in the Commons, MPs being subjected to tests of their sobriety by in-House Rozzers, such as their response to Division Bells and ability to find their Ayes and Noes with both hands. What was he trying to do, I asked him with twinkling North German directness, sell a book? Publicise some new non-alcoholic fortified wine?

He was, I reminded him with an admonitory pat on the BTM, no stranger to the Commons before he was kicked in the Upper Chamber. Why didn't the two of us stroll in to wet our Whistlers?

A welcoming committee of one, slurred of voice and crossed of eye, approached my Lord Avebury and painstakingly emptied approximately 1.35 litres of beer over his boyish head.

What would Parliamentarians say and do, our new friend argued in a pithy, undecorated English, if their mania was not to some extent muted by a sedative draft now and then? Look what happened to the former Lord Stansgate, he of the pipe and swivelling eyes, when he *stopped* drinking at 3.30 in the morning only the week before?

With the dialogue re-established, I tiptoed out, leaving

the diminutive Lord, it seemed to be in fancy, not unlike the fictional canary Tweetie-Pie in a Cathouse of salivating Pussy-cats Sylvester.

On Hearing the First Coup

It comes sometimes as a bit of an electrical shock to English colleagues, prone to write me away as a jolly old Kraut with a taste for good cigars and rum anecdotes but with not much going on his top, to learn that my wife Hildegard is connected on one side to the Duke of Edinburgh. When they discover that she is further connected through him by way of the marriage coupling to Her Majesty, and hence to the multiple quarterings of the Hanover-Saxe-Coburg-Gotha-von Rundstedt-Humperdinck, their faces fall on average by about zero comma five of a kilometre.

So it was on this Easter weekend that I found myself rolling my Old Banger – Hildegard having broken her self-imposed 100 per cent embargo on country-house weekends since an unfortunate episode some years ago at Catford – up the front of Gatcombe Manor, in cowdungspattered, birdrich Gloucestershire. This is the modest but tastefully-imposing country pad of Her Serene Highness the Princess Anne Phillipson and her dazzlingly equipped fairytale if somewhat dozy husband Mike.

Mike is nothing whatsoever if not the almost perfectly conscious host, and he was the first to appear, widely smiling and filled with apologies, when our vehicle became becalmed in some kind of tanktrap contraption just inside the main gates. Security, he explained in his wry-laconic manner, as we humped and toted our bits and bobs through the spring-blossoming countryside, was always of paramount importance. He had odd balls and every kind of nosey parka forking about in the undergrowth, he said, and you had to go down on them like a thousand kilos of bricks or you never got a moment's piece of quiet.

The houseparty turns out to be a small one, consisting of Mr and Mrs Denis Healey, the Boy Jenkinses, St John Stevas and Colonel Mad Mitch. What has brought us together? I found myself wondering as the excellent

venison stew steamed my spectacles during our Good
Friday luncheon. The whiskery dark eyebrows of Mr
Healey flickering mysteriously at the Princess's left ear,
Boy Jenkins crumbling his bread roll over her right, St
John Stevas delighting my wife Hildegard with spicy items
of upstage gossip, and Mad Mitch guffawing in short bursts
at the odd *bon mot* tossed in by Mrs Healey? I am not by
nature a jealous man, but there was something in St John
Stevas's devil-may-care flutter of the eyelashes as he
played with Hildegard's hearing aid (claiming at one point
to be receiving a transmission from Hilversum) that made
me additionally uneasy.

The mystery was not long in clearing itself up. On Friday
night, after a slap-in banquet served by frogged help in a
blaze of silver-ensconced candles, Princess Anne led Mrs
Healey, Mrs Jenkins and Hildegard, now quite beetroot-
red with delight after another barrage of St John Stevas
charm, out to powder whatever it is they powder on these
occasions. Captain Phillipson passed round the After
Eighty Mints. He had, he announced, igniting a 50-
centimetre cigar, been reading a bit out of the paper about
Uncle Dickie. A lot of people seemed a bit browned up
with Mrs Thatcher, what price a *coup*?

I was, to be entirely frank, shattered to my fundament,
and beyond. Here were three men in the middle of the
road, all of them to a bigger or smaller degree critical of the
present regime, offered a chance to stop the Tory
Juggernaut. You could have heard a bin drop. Cigar smoke
continued to rise, Stevas choked a polite cough, Healey
picked between his teeth with a silver fruit knife, and
Colonel Mitch gave our host a slow, strange look. Then
Boy Jenkins, toying with a balloonful of brandy, observed
that seizing power had always seemed to him rather a
strenuous activity and they all laughed.

What an odd climate of apathy! Captain Phillipson, I
could see, was quite cross. I took the opportunity the
following day, as I strolled out in my powder-blue Easter
Bunny outfit to join him in an Egghunt, of offering myself
as the anti-Thatcher Alternative.

Had we not been overtaken at that precise moment,
arms filled with fragile eggs, by the local Hunt performing

some kind of U-turn through the rosegarden in search of an April fox, I might well have been catapulted in a twinkling into the Seat of Power, rather than face-downwards into the Compost Bed, as was in fact the case.

Thrice Hail, Sir James!

Sic, as some wise old owl in the Classical Antiquity very perceptively observed, *transit gloria mundi. Now*! is now no longer. Sir Jimmy has pulled up his bags like the Arab and silently sauntered away.

When any great tree topples over and falls into the forest there must of course be a good deal of caffuffle, weeping, washing of teeth etcetera, not least among the various birds and little fluffy mammals who had hitherto found a refuge among its bosky branches, and our hearts must inevitably go outside to those sylvan denizens who now find themselves without support or a roof over their mouths.

It was Sir James's stated policy never to employ monkeys. If you paid peanuts, this Mao Tse-Tung of European Capital observed in one of his most famous aphorisms, that was what you were liable to get, and by the waggonload. What variety of beast he wished to employ he alas has never specified, but when the branch collapses, down must come cradle and baby, Uncle Tom Cobbler and the kitchen sink.

I bend over to no man or woman alive in my admiration for Sir Jimmy. I have known him ever since he was a little Commoner at Eton, a lithe, loose-limbed charmer with porcelain blue eyes and a roguish smile playing about all over his face, smoking a cigar the size of a baseball bat as he fondled his chips in some fashionable Gambling Hell. Over the years we have become as thick as two short planks.

Where, he must himself have been asking this week as he licks at his wounds amid pulls at his Corona Magnifico Extra Long Handrolled Cuban Cigar in some Parisian niterie, did he tread on the bananapeel? He need feel no shame! The same thought must have passed through the mind of many another martyr as he found himself being cracked on the head with a precious stone, defenestrated or in the case of Saint Sebastian used as a dartboard by a lot of hobbledehoys with crossbows. And Sir Jim should take consolation from the fact that he finds himself in such a glorious company. For make no mistakes, it is among that noble army of martyrs that this poor fellow unquestionably belongs.

Who, I ask you point and blank, could have done more? So hard did this highminded entrepreneur exert himself in responding to Sir Harold Wilson's call for Merchant Venturers that he won, under the bewitching auspices of my Lady Falkender, his knightly spurs. Rumour at the time insisted he was to become the belted Earl of Goldsmith, so selflessly had he strained his sinews through thin and thick to fulfil the Wilsonian injunctions.

Hardly had the Wilson Bandstand collapsed, however, with all the post-Callaghanian mischmasch of reproach, counter-reproach, back stabbing, front stabbing, jockeying for this and that, pulling each other in bits that must spell several centuries of trouble-free Tory government, than hop-la! Sir Jim pops up as bold as bronze sitting on the Thatcheronian right hand smirking like a pussycat who has come into the cream, a pillar of the Conservative Establishment.

Now, pursuing with the singleminded devotion of a truffle hound the Friedmanite doctrine of smashing the weak up against the wall, Sir Jim offers himself as a sacrificial victim. Having clambered (if I may briefly change my metaphors) into his multi-million pound kite, he takes it up to unbelievable heights then, like our old allies the Japanese Few, he smashes himself Kamikaze-style against the self-same wall, an inspiration to other Small Businessmen everywhere.

Be still the knockers. For this paperfolding trick, Hail Sir Jimmy, threetimes Hail!

Heads of Oak

There can have been few more soul- and heartstring-stirring sights in the history of maritime endeavour than that of the old Count Bismarck making water into a stiff breeze over the heads of our former Royal Family, bobbing up and down misty-eyed in their jollyboat. A multi-coloured illustration of this moment of flagwagging and somewhat jingoistic tumthumping hung over my little cot in our high old Hanseatic townhouse in Hamburg when I was knee-deep into a grasshopper. It was this scene that fell into my mind last week, at a time when Things Nautical have been on the bubble in Whitehall, with a tremendous impact. I refer to Mr Nott and his Comic Cuts.

My father, Karl-Esme von Ofterdingen Schubert, whose mother was a born von und zu Scharnhorst-Rollmops, ended up with a good deal of scrambled egg over his hat and shoulders as Flottenadmiral i/c the gallant little boats that were able to give Jellicoe one in the eye at Jutland. Nevertheless, he never forgot that he had begun very much at the bottoms as a powdered monkey in the old days of pith and wind when he had forged many a staunch comradeship with the horny-handed old shellfronts of Kiel and Bremerhaven.

It had been their dream to develop such industrial muscle, in terms of seawending Dreadnothings, as to knock the Royal Navy for sixes and sevens, and it was their sense of frustration in not being allowed out to do this that inevitably led to the explosion of indiscipline that was the Kiel Mutiny and subsequent hooligan Revolution of 1917–18.

One point that my father was always in agony to club into me, as he would pat me on the head with his metal hand, was that a proper Navy, all shipshaped and Hamburg fashion, was a damn good PR for a country's heavy-engineering capacity. Steam down the African Coast, he would say, blow some jolly old *entrepôt* where ships of many nations are rubbing shoulders in the basin entirely out of the water, ideally from about 30 leagues out to sea and well over the horizon, and you will be the first people the blokes down there will think of when they come to ordering lawnmowers, etc., come the reconstruction.

Ditto with our gallant U-Boats. Pick off a merchantman at 10 nautical kilometres firing your torpedoes in a choppy sea and watch the orderbooks filling up for optical lenses, ballbearings and gyroscope toys.

To say that my old Pater would be pretty hoop-a-cock over recent events in Whitehall would be to pedal in it a good deal too softly. All in all he and his messing mates of the old Northseafleet must be having a bit of a titter up their richly beringed sleeves down in Mr David Jones's Locker.

I myself, as a bit of a Johnny-Looking-Both-Ways, a Euroenthusiast marinated up to the armpits in your British Way of Life, am of course torn rather up the middle over this one. To have Jolly Jack Tars dressed fore and aft in their bumfreezers, with a Royal Marine Orchestra playing 'Oaken Hearts' in every ocean of the globe, when British Engineering is unable to deliver even the spare parts, let alone the nitty-gritty, would obviously be a farce and a waste of the Frau Führer's much-needed pennies.

Surely some token ceremonial presence, however, akin to Her Majesty's Mounted Life and Bodyguards, e.g. a highly spat and polished detachment of Sailor Boys manning HMS *Victory* refloated in the Thames, would be preferable to Mr Nott's envisaged Royal Naval establishment by 1990 of one lone Frog-Man with a Water-pistol.

Denis as Menace

'All of the world,' as your Immortal Bird expressed it in one of his pithiest utterances, 'is a bit like the stage,' and it was with a highish sense of theatrical anticipation of Thursday night that I hied myself hot-feet into the Whitehall Theatre to see the new bourgeois drama *Anyone for Tennis?*

As a West German Egg Head I have always had an extremely soft whatnot for Old Lady Thespis. Standing as we Germans do up to the back teeth in the broad mainstream of European Theatre, with its sources in the turbulent effusions of Sturm und Drang, and broadening out into the world-engulfing flood of heavy Brechtian pieces that have stunned audiences and knocked them into a heap for the past fifty years, we love nothing better than to sink into the hot red plush as the lights are extinguished and pop on our Thinkingcaps.

Here was a meaty feast for us to get our eye-teeth in. Set in present-day Britain, this deeply moving slice of High Life is tossed into our lap hot from the creative cookingpot to make of what we will. An ageing husband, Denis, finds himself with a loose end in the absence of his tough-as-old-Wellington-boots wife, Margaret, and seeks solace in the companionship of a Pinter-Beckettesque gang of alcohol-soaked derelicts, among them 'the Major' and 'Maurice', with whom he wishes to dream away the Imperial Twilight, Loss of International Prestige, the Soggy Dog-End of Life.

Alack for him, his dominant Venus in Furs of a Lady Wife throws a spanner into the mangle. She rejigs her schedules and turns up in an unexpected *coup de théâtre* in their shared matrimonial domicile, to throw a big business meeting. As he expresses his chagrin in images larded with excremental resonances, the Little Man makes desperate efforts to conceal the very existence of his down-and-out chums, one of whom symbolically wears an ill-fitting

164

National Health toupée, and is, significantly, shut *into a closet*.

It does not take a Jung or a Christopher Booker to spot that the dramatist is putting his finger into the shadowside of the husband's existence. From now on, any literary critic worth his salt will be alerting the rest of his row in the audience to what our author is actually trying to say. Could it be a coincidence, I inquired of my fellow theatregoers in a forceful whisper, that the names of both husband and wife happened to be those of the Prime Minister and her publicity-shunning Consort? The fact that I was instantly biffed over the nut with a duck-handled sunshade by some Philistine in the seat behind for doing so did not deter me from my quest.

Here, surely, is a dark Ibsenesque metaphor of late Twentieth-Century Britain. The wife Margaret is *anima*, a looker on life with the sunnyside up, an interfering old bag, call her what you will. She is attempting to bring order to the Unconscious, in this case represented by the National Health toupée-wearer who has had a drop too much to drink and flaked up on the carpet.

As is often the case, this bright Appolonian ideal soon runs into some pretty choppy water. Despite the cooperation of a butler, Jenkins – clearly an allusion to Jung's pupil Dr Otto 'Nicely, Nicely' Jenkins who ran a lucrative practice in St John's Wood until disappearing to South America in 1951 – the *anima* figure Margaret fails to untangle the dark chaos.

We recognise the eternal interplay between light and dark, overworld and underworld, drunken sleep and wakeful hopping about, dim Little Englandism and the Bright European Future. In a deeply moving climax, the derelicts re-appear, purged and ransomed, in female attire, indistinguishable, give or take a moustache or so, from the Dominant Margaret.

And who is it who leads these Eurydices up from the Depths? A charming, bright-eyed Pan, a Hamburger to boot, rejoicing, I may say to my intense delight, in the same name as myself, Herr Schubert. The concept of a German Orpheus, all bitterness forgotten, leading these Doppelgänger-Britannias out of the appalling mess in which they find themselves, I see as a lambent gleam of European Hope, Forgiveness and Reconciliation.

That most of the audience seemed to laugh derisively throughout I can only interpret as further proof of what a howling cultural wilderness of apes has always existed in these islands.

Idle Splashing

The Matchstick Man

The first time I heard Billy Graham was on a stuffy summer afternoon in Eastbourne in 1954.

He had, at that stage, not yet made the Big Time. We were, I think, about thirty souls in all, in thick grey flannel trousers and tweed jackets, all holding in our moist hands two soft-covered books of *CSSM Choruses*, a hymn book called *Golden Bells* and a Bible. Dominating us from behind a table covered with thick green cloth were the three leaders of the Eastbourne Crusaders' Bible Class for Boys: Mr Prentice, in a brown suit, who worked in a bank, Dr Snowball, in blue, and Mr Grey, a local dentist, in a dark suit, with a forbiddingly lined face, thick glasses, and a clipped bristly moustache. After the long afternoons of tedium during which we were threatened with the imminent dissolution of the planet, or at best the establishment of Russian concentration camps all over England within the next five years, it was an unspeakable relief to be entertained by an American in a pale blue lightweight suit demonstrating the intricacies of metaphysics with a box of matches and a clean white handkerchief.

His first trick illustrated to our adolescent minds the efficacy of prayer. Striking a match and holding it up between an eloquent thumb and forefinger, with a dazzling white cuff against the supple brown wrist and the blue eyes blazing beneath his heavy brows, he likened the match to a soul 'newly afyah with love for Gohd'. Watching the flame swaying and shrinking on the upright white stick, he drew our attention to its waning power. The flame of enthusiasm was growing weaker: 'But friends, the Biable says that those who wait upon tha Lohad shull re-new theyah strength. By kneeling down befoah Gohd in prayah.' He tipped the match, so that the burnt end was downmost, and behold, the flame revived and bloomed on the blackened stick. He then blew it out and went on to his next point.

The second miracle required the handkerchief and two matches. Slipping one match discreetly into the hem, the Evangelist held the handkerchief out at arm's length in his left hand and flapped it deftly to demonstrate that it was empty. Then he brought forward the second match in his right hand and explained that this, too, represented a human soul, pure and white and perfect as it had been before the Fall, ready to burn with the fire of God. Having explained this, he covered the match with the handkerchief, arranging it in his left hand so that the outline of the match was still apparently visible. A volunteer was called up from the audience, an awkward boy with round glasses who held his head on one side, and the Illusionist asked him to verify by feeling the stick that this was indeed the true match.

When he had done this and nodded, the Preacher turned to us once again. No soul, he said, was perfect: no soul since the Fall of Man could have any part in the power or love of God. 'For all have sinned an' come short of the gloreah of Gohd, Romans Three, Twenty-Three. An' the wages of seeyan' – he dwelt with particular stress on that mystical word – 'is Death.' Taking over for a moment the role of the angry Jehovah in Judgment, the boy with the round spectacles followed the Evangelist's instructions, took the matchstick beneath the handkerchief, and snapped it. The Preacher thanked his assistant and asked him to return to his seat. 'An' yet mah friends,' he continued, 'Gohd so loved the world, John's Gospel, Chapter Three and Verse Sixteen, that he gayve his Only Begotten Son that whosoevah be-leeveth in Him might not perish but have Everlasting Life.' And shaking out his handkerchief he produced for our inspection the matchstick, miraculously restored. Dr Graham went on to apply the parable to each individual, recalling impure thoughts and deeds of shame, and appealing for a total surrender to

Christ as the Way, the Truth, and the Life, without whom no soul could be re-united with God.

Since then I've understood the trick, but I'm still confused by the theology.

On the Run

During our National Service we were taught what was called Escape and Evasion. The training, it is true, concentrated more on developing our evasive tendencies than on the actual mechanics of sawing through an iron bar or sliding down a silken cord, but it is nevertheless worth while at a time like this reminding the taxpayer that even now future escapees are being coached at his expense in new techniques that will mystify the police and elicit gasps of admiration from the newspapers in some future escape drama.

Our instructions began in conditions of maximum security behind a high perimeter fence, topped with barbed wire, in a battle camp in North Wales. We were surrounded on every side by high green hills with outcrops of grey rock and tumbled stone walls, silent except for the bleating of grubby grey sheep which we shot at with light machine-guns and rifles, with great enthusiasm but little apparent effect, on those rare occasions when we were allowed out of the camp to make the valleys echo on a live-firing exercise. We stood to attention in a damp Nissen hut, crop-headed and wearing overalls suggesting some less enlightened forced-labour scheme in Siberia, and were asked to sit down please by a nice officer in the Gurkhas with slightly prominent front teeth and a black moustache.

Laying his leather gloves on the table, he explained that the object of this exercise was to avoid capture, and to break through a strong cordon of watchful security guards, assisted by the local constabulary, who would be surrounding the camp. Other patrols would be scouring the hills searching for us, and if we were not back by nightfall we should have failed. The security patrols would then presumably start scouring the hills in deadly earnest. We were to be issued with haversack rations, a map of the area and a compass, and would be dropped somewhere within a twelve-mile radius of the camp. We were encouraged to disguise ourselves, and to make use of our fieldcraft and crawls. We should be working in pairs. If there were no questions, the convoy would move off.

It was only when we were sitting in the three-ton lorry, watching the green-grey landscape dwindling behind us, that the hopelessness of our task began to become apparent. Dressed as we were in heavy hobnailed boots, army overalls, belts and berets, we realised the impracticability of the more exciting possibilities suggested by escape stories of the last war. Theatrical costumiers were rare in that part of Wales, and the more generous countryfolk who might out of the goodness of their hearts have provided us with odds and ends out of Granny's dressing-up trunk had become alarmed at the sudden explosion of erratically-aimed mortar bombs and ill-advised bursts of machine-gun fire, and had for the most part moved away. It also struck us that pairs of curiously dressed grannies in big army boots clambering over barbed-wire fences high up in the hills might alert the suspicions of even the black-moustached Gurkha officer with the prominent teeth. Certainly subtleties like forged passports and an authentic Welsh accent, we decided, as the truck stopped to let us climb out in some deserted lane, were out of the question.

We were sitting under a hedge by the roadside, eating our thick corned-beef sandwiches and looking out gloomily over the wet open countryside that descended gently to our objective round a bend in the valley, when a local policeman bicycled up. He wished us good day. We discussed the weather, and he asked us if we were from the camp then. We said we were, and he leaned on his bicycle and said we have a fair amount of running about to do, he imagined. We agreed that we had. He showed some interest in our haversack rations, observed that man could not live by bread alone, as they say, and that he must go and have his dinner. He then pedalled away down the road and was soon lost to sight. Immensely encouraged at our ice-cold nerve and evasiveness, we set off walking down the road after him, occasionally turning, when we heard a car behind us, to thumb a lift, but without success.

Far away, up in the hills, we occasionally caught sight of

pairs of tiny figures, scrambling among the wet rocks, but otherwise the countryside was peaceful, and it was difficult to believe that we were actually on the run. The weather, I remember, suddenly improved halfway through the afternoon, and when we reached the next little village the slate roofs were all shining in the sunshine, there was a blue sky over the green valley, and it was all very agreeable.

We stopped at the local post office and sent off a few picture postcards, and then to our great surprise found a tea-shop, with a quiet back room with a carpet on the floor and white cloths on the tables, and a little window with a distant view of the hills. We had tea and hot scones and butter, talked for some reason about romantic poetry, and lay about smoking cigarettes in the manner of undergraduates on a late-nineteenth-century walking tour. The fact that we were dressed in overalls and large boots seemed only to add to the feeling of stolen pleasure, and we were extremely reluctant to leave. Fortunately, we were then joined by two others who had been clambering about in the wet grass and were equally delighted to find this little asylum, and the jokes and light literary conversation continued until late in the afternoon when the sun was beginning to go down.

Sticking to their theory that the only safe route was to avoid the main roads, the others set off across a high sloping field, and we continued along the road between the dry stone walls. Almost immediately a car overtook us, and stopped. He could not take us very far, he said, as he was only going down to the army camp to deliver some stuff for the NAAFI. We got in, and were just approaching the camp when we saw in the distance that two NCOs were flagging the car down, indicating that it should pull in. We both slid down behind the driver's seat, told him to pay no attention to the irresponsible practical jokers at the roadside, and were let out a few moments later at the back door of the NAAFI. If it is of any comfort to the police, it was only after double egg, chips and beans that we discovered we were the only ones to get through.

In Old Japan

One of the most fundamental mistakes made by travel writers, it seems to me, is that they still believe we are interested in reading about something 'different'. In spite of the fact that every modern traveller experiences the opposite, they still persist in giving the impression that everything beyond the horizon is 'strange' or 'foreign', 'typical' of some ancient and exotic culture that is quite alien to our own. Far better for the travel writers to accept reality as it is, and to enthuse instead about the wonderful sameness awaiting the traveller abroad.

I stumbled on this truth some years ago when I was travelling in Japan. All the traditional shrines of Japanese culture – theatres, baths, brothels and temples – seemed to be thronged with European visitors, and as I was anyway short of money and had been away from England for almost a year it struck me, sitting among the guidebooks in Tokyo, that the ideal place to go would be a pub in Kobe called 'The Red Lion'. The guidebook also mentioned a place called the Kobe Club, where English colonels could be seen drinking pink gin and playing dominoes. I cabled my bank in London to transfer a meagre sum to Kobe, and set off immediately by train.

The journey itself was uneventful, except for the arrival in the doorway of the compartment of a sales girl, apparently selling boxes of chocolate. I selected a rather nice-looking box with a picture of some mountains and a lake on the front, showed the sales girl some coins, a few of which she took, and settled back in my seat to unwrap the goodies. I was aware almost immediately of those opposite looking at me with their impassive almond eyes, but paid no attention and went on trying to undo the tight cellophane wrapping. The packet seemed to be made of light tin, and when the lid finally came off I was surprised to find it contained only flat strips of dried seaweed. I looked up at the four pairs of attentive and still impassive almond eyes, affected a quietly triumphant smirk to suggest that the packet contained after all what I expected, shut the lid, put it into a paper bag with the rest of my belongings, and looked out of the window.

I was not surprised after that to find when I arrived in Kobe that it was the Emperor's birthday and that all the banks were shut. I was also not entirely certain where the English bank had transferred the money to, but after a walk through the colourful streets, where the soldiers mutilated in the war had been brought out in hundreds in yellow uniforms with the red star in the cap to beg in the gutter, I found a bank with a plate beside the door saying that they were agents for my own bank in England. The front doors were shut, but a door round the side had been left open, and I went in, hoping to meet someone who might be able to speak English. It was deserted. I was some way in among the clutter of little desks behind the main counter, innocently searching for some list or notice that might give me the name of the British representative, when I heard a sharp exclamation, presumably in Japanese, from behind me in the doorway. I looked round and found a man in semi-military uniform pointing a gun at me.

After some moments of misunderstanding it emerged that he spoke pidgin English, and he immediately became more charming. He put his gun away, explained that he had learned English while working as a pirate in Hong Kong, and insisted that I should come up to his nightwatchman's room for a drink. He had just bought an electric mixer, and he poured in a tin of orange juice and a bottle of saki and turned it on. He showed me a piece of his pirate boat, which he had been blown up in by the Japanese air force during the war, and a Union Jack-draped portrait of King George VI, for whom he apparently had great affection. We then drank the saki and orange – he prefaced each glass by remarking 'God Save the Queen' – I thanked him, and found my way out into the street.

'The Red Lion' was shut. I had a look through the keyhole at all the English chairs and tables, and then set off extravagantly in a taxi for the Kobe Club. True to life, they were all sitting there playing dominoes and drinking pink gin. I ordered the same, and settled down contentedly to listen to the familiar cadences and the restful click of the dominoes. After a few moments one of the colonels got up from his game and came over. I explained that I was in the army, had got a lift from Seoul on an American aeroplane, had left my uniform with friends in Tokyo and come down to Kobe in my only suit of civilian clothes and a paper bag containing, among other things, a tin of seaweed, to visit the British pub.

He listened to my story about the bank, seemed sympathetic, and suggested very helpfully that I might like to stay in one of the guest rooms of the club until the money came through. He would, however, have to confer with the committee. The committee, six or seven kindly old men in blazers and silk squares, then literally went into a huddle over by the window, from time to time casting a glance in my direction, and I sat as nonchalantly as possible at the bar looking into space. In the end, one of them came back and said he'd never heard such nonsense in his life and would I get out immediately. You couldn't get much samer than that.

Up with the Lark

Mr Anthony Chenevix-Trench, the tiny but ebullient headmaster of Eton, appears to have caused a mild rumpus among Old Etonian elements in the afternoon drinking clubs and labour exchanges by announcing the abolition of Early School. This, it is perhaps necessary to explain for progressive readers, was the first lesson of the day at Eton, beginning at seven-thirty and ending at eight-fifteen, when the little inmates were released for breakfast. It was, he felt, unreasonable to expect boys on cold winter mornings to go straight into classrooms 'without even a cup of tea'. There was, however, no mention in the handout of the wretched ushers, to whom even a cup of tea was no great incentive – that dim band of workers who were described by Wayland Young, I think, as the boys' 'intellectual lackeys'.

I first went into service there myself in the autumn of 1961. The only warning I had received of Early School was from a retired beak living on the south coast, who said that he had always found it an awe-inspiring ordeal, and had made a habit of being in his bath by six-thirty in order to prepare himself for it. This struck me at the time as being a little over-cautious, but I was nevertheless in the bath by seven on the first morning, even risking the depressive effect of having to share the bathroom with a fresh-faced and hearty young colleague who chattered away brightly while shaving, and I lay boss-eyed and groaning in the bath. The only interesting feature of his toilet was that he filled the basin with hot water and then left the taps running, so that water was constantly overflowing into the waste-pipe. In this way he could dip his razor into the water near the outlet, the little pieces of shaving soap and stubble were carried away, and the rest of the water remained pure. He himself was unable to explain why he did it, but I discussed it with his aunt some time later, and she said

176

she thought it almost certainly had some psychological explanation.

Despite these distractions, I had tied my white tie by seven-twenty-five, drunk my cup of tea, gathered up my books and my gown, and was ready to unfold the riches of *Faust, Part 1*, to my new masters. In prospect, the idea of Early School on a bright September morning was not unattractive. Everything in Eton always has a scrubbed and well-cared-for look about it, and with the sun on the old red brick, a blue, peaceful morning sky over the meadows and the birds singing, it all seemed rather nice. The boys slouched along in their black theatrical costumes with a certain gawky elegance, spruce young masters marched down to their schoolrooms with an air of selfconscious cockiness, one rigid white finger extended to keep their bright new briefcases shut, and older masters glided pacifically past on rusty bicycles, occasionally exposing a few yellowing dentures in a humourless leer of greeting. It was possible to feel oneself a part of some timeless academic pageant, going down to drink at dawn from the pure fount of all wisdom. Inside the schoolroom, these illusions evaporated. Grey-faced and still sticky with sleep, twenty-five children in shiny black tailcoats and grubby white ties dragged themselves to their feet and then flopped back in attitudes suggesting nausea or penitential gloom, mingled in some cases with a hint of feeble contempt. The idea of kindling any flame of interest seemed as ridiculous as striking a match under water.

To begin with, the challenge nevertheless seemed irresistible. Leaning out of the leaded window overlooking an orchard and a quiet cottage garden, I would inhale huge draughts of morning-chilled air, and then pace up and down dictating copious notes on Goethe's imagery and symbolism. The decadently sloping lids grew heavier, and the ink-stained fingers moved slowly across the page. Information seemed to be seeping in, but only through a drugged haze. I tried sudden and exaggeratedly dramatic readings from the original, representing Faust as a mixture between Sir Laurence's Richard III and Robert Newton's Long John Silver. ('Come 'ere, Mephistopheles, lad.') Hands were thrust almost elbow-deep into trouser pockets, and heads nodded nearer to the desks. I even tried telling jokes. Next door, the voice of my nearest fellow-lackey droned on like the chanting of some unenthusiastic Buddhist recluse, and I began to realise that sooner or later I should have to surrender to the system.

The theory held by most of the staff seemed to be that Early School was tolerable, as it offered the opportunity of hitting them when they were groggy. Later on in the day they would have woken up and started applying their minds to new schemes for spreading treacle on the seat of one's armchair or for locking the French master in the lavatory. Before breakfast they were passive and malleable. Even if this had been true, the task of moulding minds at that time of the morning became less and less attractive as November deepened into December. The mornings grew darker and more arctic, hoar-frost gleamed on the roads, and breath, even in the schoolrooms, seemed to hang about like fog. I delayed getting up more and more, waiting first until my fresh-faced colleague had finished splashing about in the bathroom, and then until he had gone downstairs before I turned back the warm covers and began to grope about in the darkness for the plug of the electric fire.

Usually I managed to stumble down to the schoolrooms just behind the last little lord, who would be holding up his trousers with one hand and trailing his braces, while I peered at my books in the icy darkness to see if I had brought the right ones. In some cases I had not, and the forty-five minutes was spent in elaborate evasions. The only real breakthrough occurred on the last morning before the Christmas holidays, when a boy called Duckworth, who had been scattering metaphorical marbles under my feet for some weeks, put his hand up and said that it was a tradition on the last morning at Early School to embark upon community singing. Fighting down my feelings of hunger, fatigue and rage, I said that it sounded a nice idea and perhaps he would like to conduct. As I watched the vile infant struggling to overcome the sleepy apathy and natural reserve of his little chums as they joined in 'Jonah rowed the boat ashore', it occurred to me that it was probably the most worthwhile Early School I had ever attended, and the singing even succeeded in drowning the earnest monotone from next door. How wise of A. C. Trench to cut it off for ever.

Little Victims

In the days when I was a beak there, I had rather mixed feelings about Eton on the Fourth of June. On that date, or nowadays on the nearest convenient Saturday, the boys' parents and sisters come down, as every gossip columnist knows, to hear speeches, visit various exhibitions, and watch a cricket match on the great playing field, celebrated in song and story, called Agar's Plough.

On the one hand the theatrical spectacle, culminating in quaint activities on the river at dusk and a gigantic firework display, was irresistible: on the other, like a dance performed by the burglar anxious to pass himself off as an authentic guest at the hunt ball when the spoons and forks begin to cascade out of his sleeves and fall with an unseemly clang and clatter on the polished floor, it should have been stopped, if only for the school's own good.

The distinction between Upstairs and Downstairs at Eton is one not easily glossed over. Anyone unwise enough to refer to the Young Masters would be left in no doubt as to whom the term referred. Our noble little employers might 'cap' us – raising preferably any other combination than two fingers to their now no longer existent top hats when they passed us in the street – but we were well aware that our true place was behind the green baize door, somewhere above the butler and somewhere below the man from Christie's who came to value the pictures.

I suppose I was luckier than some, in that I was known to have appeared at the opening night of the Establishment Club and got back in time for Early School at seven-thirty the next morning, and to contribute to a newly founded satirical magazine. But this also had its disadvantages: various successful attempts were made by my lustre-lending friends in London to embarrass me – the entire editorial staff of *Private Eye* hired a horse-drawn vehicle from Windsor Station and behaved appallingly in Eton

High Street. I received letters addressed to me at the School Office prominently marked 'if undelivered please return to the British League of Homosexuals, Cable Street, Slough', and, after one holiday engagement in cabaret at Ilford, the *Daily Mail* ran a leading article saying 'Eton Master Peddles Smut in East End' and demanding that I should be sacked.

But as far as the boys were concerned, beaks were beaks, and it was little consolation to be present when two members of Pop – a mutual appreciation society for boys in the Sixth Form who are allowed to wear embroidered waistcoats with their Little Undertaker outfits – sprawling on the sofa of a colleague who was himself an Old Etonian and a member of an ancient and noble family, described him, as he left the drawing room for a moment to fetch them a drink, as 'such a ghastly middle-class little man'. We were all ghastly middle-class little men, and we accepted it.

Nevertheless, huddled in the equivalent of the Servants' Hall – the bachelor masters' 'colonies' or the married staff's cautiously furnished homes – we dressed each morning in a similar uniform to that worn by our betters – in our case a charcoal grey suit fraying at the cuffs, yellowing celluloid stick-up collar and a rust-stained made-up white bow tie – and dreamed our dreams of petty bourgeois grandeur, meeting at night to tell familiar old jokes – 'You tell it, Kelsall!', 'No, no, Richard, you tell it *so* much better!' – all of which seemed to end with some fellow-menial in an MA gown being called 'Sir' by a Viscount.

On the Fourth of June any such phantom consolations were cruelly dispelled. The sheer weight of money on Agar's Plough hit you like a wall of liquid platinum. Who Agar was and what he did with his Plough I never discovered: presumably he was driven off, patronised and condescended to, by the first Fourth of Juners ever, advancing in their braying waves from ranks of golden carriages, the historical equivalent of today's rows of glittering Rolls-Royces, laden down with hampers and champagne, every last axle-bolt breathed on and buffed up by a uniformed chauffeur. But the field now seemed to burn a brilliant green against the old red brick of the school as if every blade of grass had been placed there by an art director and lit by a privately hired sun: tens of thousands of pounds' worth of cosmetic dentistry flashed California white, toupees blown and coaxed into perfection by exorbitant French wigmakers, every fragile summer hat and long white glove, every button-hole and square inch of polished leather hand-stitched and fussed over regardless of expense.

For the teaching staff it was Waterloo, standing there like tramps in the middle of a major production of *Der Rosenkavalier* at Covent Garden.

But the economic give-away was not just the immediate vulgar extravagance, it was the dramatic manner in which it reflected those unseen millions of pounds spent over the years since old Agar fled to Slough on transforming the foul-mouthed, swivel-eyed cut-throats – great-great-grandfathers, grandfathers, or in some cases obviously fathers of present Etonians – into that perfect fashion parade, chins raised and implacably confident, that takes the field today.

It would be tempting to summon up the spectre of spiritual or emotional impoverishment, hollow-eyed and rattling its begging bowl, behind every well-fed infant as they pace across the green: but there is more distressing evidence to be seen in reality. Double chins beginning to show in some young Tweedledum in a short jacket and a deep collar, or a member of Pop, inherited deformities apart, loping along with all the dignity of a self-made man of seventy: as if, having been bombarded with particles of bullion since conception, he had become a gold-plated image of premature self-satisfaction, all ambition fulfilled, with nowhere to go but down.

The Show Goes On

I think it is quite possible that the Royal Tournament at Earls Court may very soon become Outrageously High Camp. It is obviously regarded as that already by the shadowy male frails who flit about in the darkened galleries waiting to wave to the sailors, but for the rest of the adults in the audience it remains a children's entertainment. They sit there among the shrill screaming of the wolf cubs and the uninhibited enthusiasm of their own children bouncing up and down among their knees with terrible expressions of melancholy half-detached embarrassment, waiting for it to be over. But by the time the grave beards, experimental theatre lovers and society beauties move in the audience may well find that they are not watching a children's entertainment at all, but a shatteringly dramatic collage of pop that shakes their preconceived ideas about the theatre to the very foundations.

There is one moment about halfway through the show which seems to me of particular significance where a Royal Navy Diving and Bomb Disposal Squad are lowered from a rubber canoe suspended just under the roof down into the darkened but ultra-violet-lit arena. The illusion of submarine activity is created in fairly broad strokes with the use of pale green octopuses, orange rays and yellow starfish which all glow with ultra-violet radiance in the blackness. The shirts and summer dresses of the audience also glow, so the effect is not without a certain charm. The bomb disposal expert is then seen groping his way on the end of a luminous rope across the floor of the arena towards what is described by the commentator as a dangerous unexploded mine. The expert kneels down beside the glowing green drum in the darkness, mimes a few tinkering movements to amplified clanks and bangs on the soundtrack, and then the commentator, who sounds exactly like Kenneth Horne, tells us that he has set off the fuse, and that he has only fifteen seconds left. The seconds begin to tick away in the soundtrack, the expert mimes further tinkering, and then on the fourteenth second stands back and the ticking stops. Kenneth Horne gives a gasp of unbelieving admiration and says, 'He's done it!' and the children break into applause.

Now the importance of this incident, which from the point of view of theatrical impact is one of the weakest in the whole show, is that everyone knows it is not a real mine, and yet they are applauding the man's achievement in disarming it. At another stage in the demonstration the Royal Air Force let off a toy missile, which rockets away up towards the ceiling leaving a trail of sparks and is then picked up on a film screen in colour, seen to converge on an approaching jet bomber, and to explode in a bloom of orange flame. The applause then is for the ingenuity of the spectacle. In the case of the luminous mine the applause is for the drama: the actor and the commentator succeed in convincing the audience that what he is doing is true, even though they know rationally that it is not.

And yet this effect has been achieved with theatrical devices unquestionably less powerful than anything else in the show. The ultra-violet light, used only in this sequence, makes the audience more aware rather than less aware of the simple theatrical apparatus, and despite that they allow themselves to be taken in by the conjuring trick. What we are left with the rest of the time are a series of powerful dynamic images, all of them charged with strong historical associations, violent and full of danger, but entirely abstract, having no ultimate dramatic climax, no story to tell, no hero and no development.

The Royal Navy field gun competition gives us the brawny lads in the white leggings humping huge pieces of dismantled guns over walls, sliding across wires on pulleys, scrambling over more barriers and then dropping them with a great three-ton thump to assemble them again, form up round the gun and fire three rounds: the movement and the energy are as gripping and exhilarating as the wildest sea-battle in the epic cinema, and yet we are conscious all the time that the rough backcloth at one end of the arena showing a city wall and the distant colonial landscape is only decoration, unconnected with what is going on, and that all the involvement of the audience is disciplined into sympathising with one team or the other in a formalised race.

Similarly the spectacle of the massed pipes and drums of the Lowland and Highland Brigades, with the patterns of blue and green and red-black plaids, the spinning white drumsticks and the flash of silver clasps brings the level of sentimental suspension of disbelief among the audience to such a pitch that any story told against it would be accepted without a flicker of criticism: but there is no story. The gymnastic display hypnotises the eye with the flowering and unfolding of patterns as fifty impersonal and perfectly controlled dummies in red and white roll outwards from the centre and roll inwards again, others dive across the central platform like streaks of pure white colour split second after split second, but the spectacle has no meaning beyond the perfection of the discipline. The King's Troop of the Royal Horse Artillery cross and re-cross the arena, three pairs of horses to each smoothly spinning gun carriage, harnesses jingling and glinting, toy soldiers in plumes and frogged tunics, but never coming to relieve any beleaguered garrison, only creating patterns.

What makes these abstract elements of a spectacular drama even more impressive out of any context is their unselfconscious heritage of ancient pop: drums and trumpets that once stirred the feelings to roaring exhilaration, silencing the reason and sending men out to a hot-blooded death, uniforms like theatrical costumes designed to increase the human stature from a confused reflective individual to a single-minded symbol of aggressive power, the creative rituals that once welded many men into a single weapon, still surviving in a peaceful corner of the napalm and electronic war like the colourful rituals of a forgotten religion or the treasures of a ruined church. I suppose that those who have organised the Tournament could be under the illusion that the show will drive the audience mad enough to enlist in Britain's dwindling divisions. Failing that it's fairly good as subsidised theatre.

Table for One

I have always found a kind of excruciating pleasure in sitting alone in restaurants. It may be that the unnatural act of eating solo in public heightens the sensibilities to an unusual degree, but the most trivial conversations conducted *sotto voce* at the next table, the most ordinary tie-fingering inquiries about a table for three, the simplest slapstick with spaghetti or grapefruit, or the poignant sadness of anyone else eating alone all take on the nature of dramatic entertainment. It is as impossible to read a book or pursue an independent train of thought as it would be in the theatre, and behind the feeble pretence of reading the small print on the mineral water bottle or looking innocently into the middle distance, one involuntarily strains for the next line, and the mind is poised to throw itself into rapturous applause or laughter.

This obviously has its disadvantages. Boring conversations that are obviously boring the participants only slightly or not at all can bore the silent spectator to the point of fury. Ingenuous indiscretions about mutual acquaintances run on unchecked, reducing the listener at another table to exaggerated frenzies of coughing, pepper-grinding, and chair-shifting, and however ham-handed the efforts of the elderly seducer, the rejected mistress, the precocious godchild or the moustachioed wit may be, the unseen audience, as in the theatre, is powerless to intervene. The activity is not without its dangers, either, as I realised one evening after listening with growing rage to the fatuous monologue of a middle-aged American tourist from Wyoming, whom I attempted to silence with a malign glare. He appeared to pay no attention, and then as he was leaving he whispered to his wife, 'Hey, did you see that faggot over there? He was eyeing me up all evening.'

There are, however, moments of compensation. As for example one day last week when I decided to have an early lunch in order to read a script. I had hardly read the first few lines when a knowledgeable, well-informed business voice began to impose itself, informing us that the speaker had experienced some reluctance on the part of the planning authority to authorise the erection of a caravan park in addition to a car port. I did my best to concentrate on the script, but I realised it was useless and settled back to listen to the difficulties he had had in extending the concrete surfacing from the party wall to the main wall adjoining the house. It was a small and rather exotic Mexican restaurant, and the narrator, a plump man in a grey suit accompanied by two other fifty-year-olds, seemed a little out of place among the decor of bulls' heads, guitars and Mexican rustic furniture.

The narrator, it seemed, had only recently purchased the caravan, but was more than satisfied with it, especially as it contained a built-in toilet unit. His daughter apparently had developed such an aversion to continental toilets that she had returned from their last holiday in Spain severely constipated. During this exposition it was possible for the audience – consisting of two Mexican waiters and myself, sitting in the opposite corner of the restaurant – to learn about the character and background of the speaker, and of his two rather soft-voiced companions, who seemed to fulfil the role of courtiers, only occasionally daring to offer murmurs of admiration and agreement. One of them did attempt at one point to brag about his own holiday accom- modation on the Costa del Sol, but he was rapidly crushed by the main character threatening to rent it from him. With the exposition complete, it seemed almost certain that we were in for a one-act experiment in the theatre of tedium.

Then suddenly the tone of the voice changed. He told them that he was going to set them a little problem. The problem had been devised by the Manchester School of Business Management, and was designed to test the ability of business executives to deduce facts from given situa- tions. A man opens the door of a room and looks inside. He sees a man of exactly the same height as himself lying on the bed with a piece of wood. The piece of wood has a little bit missing from one end. The first man laughs and goes out. What is the situation?

The creatures of his whim were then forced to ask questions. Both appeared reluctant. Gradually, however, the more powerful character imposed itself and they miserably asked how long the piece of wood was, how tall the man who had come in was, and why he was lying on the bed. Clearly very pleased, the main character told them that they were not allowed to ask questions like that, but only questions requiring the answer yes or no. Even more miserably they inquired whether it was a long piece of wood, whether the person lying on the bed was a tall person, whether it had been a sardonic laugh or an amused laugh. This almost floored the main character, who thought that it might have been a sardonic laugh, but decided in the end it had been an amused laugh. One of the courtiers tried tragically to break away by engaging in conversation with the waiter, but he was dragged back.

Despite attempts to give up, they were forced to continue the questioning for almost twenty minutes. The dialogue closely resembled Beckett's. Finally he revealed that the man on the bed was a dwarf. Until that morning he had believed he was the shortest man in the world. Another dwarf of exactly the same height had then challenged him to a competition. Before the competition, however, the other dwarf had secretly entered the room and cut a little piece off the first dwarf's metre stick. The first dwarf had measured himself with it, believed that he had grown, and committed suicide. The rival dwarf had then opened the door, seen him lying on the bed dead with the sawn-off metre-stick, and had laughed. The courtiers appeared stunned. To complete the carnage, the main character then told an interminable story about a circus manager who had hired five Basque dwarf acrobats, accommodated them for some reason at the Regent Palace Hotel, and allowed them to get drunk with some people in the bar who spoke French, stand on each other's shoulders and run through the revolving door where they had met with an accident. The moral of the story, he told them, was that you shouldn't put all your Basques in one exit. And who wants the Grand Guignol, ducky, when you can get that?

Love in the Park

Hyde Park, after the rain last Saturday afternoon, seemed shockingly green and innocent. The usual thick carpet of loons making love underfoot had vanished – presumably because the grass was still too wet to writhe on in comfort – and in the sunlight under the trees Indian families with gentle brown eyes sat in their deck chairs, talking. Beside the Serpentine, where dinghies with full red and white sails turned to black silhouettes against the golden glare of the sun on the water, there were more families: Dutch and Japanese, French, and American husbands in Bavarian hats and with white-painted push-chairs, all suggesting a technicolor propaganda film intended to illustrate the carefree racial harmony that exists in our beautiful and cosmopolitan capital city on the banks of the Thames. In fact it was so cosmopolitan that I didn't hear a single English voice until I had crossed the park and came to Speakers' Corner.

There were only two speakers to be seen, and by far the larger crowd had gathered around a heavily built West Indian in a tweed jacket and a waterproof black hat. He spoke slowly – perhaps because few of his audience appeared to speak or understand English, being for the most part Scandinavian – and with great authority, weighing his pauses and phrases, and emphasising his points with a blunt jab of his forefinger. 'And when that black man,' he was saying, 'heard the music of love and acceptance he stepped forward and he embraced Mao Tse-Tung. And again people saw what the Anglo-Saxon would call a humorous spectacle, a black man hugging up a Chinese man. But those people did not laugh, because they had not been indoctrinated in racial prejudice.'

Some fifty yards away a lanky figure was standing with his legs apart, his long red hair blowing into his face, and reading to a smaller crowd from a book of poetry. His voice was flat and monotonous. 'And there is a time to hate, and there is a time to love. There is a time to keep silent, and there is a time to speak. And two more government scientists threw in their sponges. Misdirected sexual energy. For is this cooling-off period to spin us out for ever? How about some love in a cool, cool climate? How about some instant joy? Ineffective sexual energy. Let's get hot again, baby. I didn't say shoot I said fuck. I'm sorry, officer, don't take me away' – the two officers about ten yards away were too busy explaining a map to a child to bother – 'I'm sorry, Mother, that's the only word that works. It's a word of love, Daddy.' Even the most studious of the Swedish hitch-hikers seemed to tire of this after a little, and began to drift back to the larger crowd where the West Indian was looking round with his slightly bloodshot eyes, holding his audience and, despite the language problem, clearly in command.

He had turned to the origins of racial prejudice, and to illustrate his point an accomplice was moving among the crowd, distributing sweets to the children. 'When I go to Northern Germany, and I reach a little farming village, or I reach to Scandinavia, where of course the people are whiter than the Americans, whiter than you – you don't see many black-haired Latin types up there – and when a woman asks me "Can I pass my hand through your hair?" she does that because of the attraction of something that is basically different.' More people on the fringes of the crowd began to pay attention at this, and the poet, realising that most of his audience was gone, suddenly turned over several pages and launched into a more modern poem which seemed to be written in the form of an auto-hypnotic incantation. It included a rising scale of nasal droning noises and hee-haws and was effective in bringing back most of his audience, who roared with laughter, clapped, and attempted to follow the text over his shoulder.

The West Indian speaker remained unruffled, replacing his hat low over his forehead and resting his hands once again on his hips in an attitude of easy confidence. 'And when I walk in the street in Sweden, and a little child runs up and looks at me, and runs after me, there is honesty in that. It isn't like when a little child in this town or in New

York is walking down the street with his mother and father or her mother and father, and a black man is coming on the other side; there isn't the unconscious indoctrination of the child by the tightening of his father's grip on his hand. You don't have to speak to indoctrinate people.'

His accomplice emerged from the thick of the crowd. He was dressed in a black suit with a black Homburg, and was without the fingers of his right hand, having only the knuckles grown over with dry grey skin. His left hand was covered with a glove, and in this he supported a paper bag full of sweets, from which some of the children nearby helped themselves and thanked him. He was, however, being pestered by a young Chinese student in a green parka, no doubt drawn in by the earlier references to Chairman Mao, with the beginnings of a stringy black beard and a fixed mocking smile, who constantly followed him asking for sweets. Finally the negro turned on him. 'Please show a little respect at least. A man is a man for all that, even though he is a louse.' The Chinese student laughed a lot more, hugging the plump English girl he was with and showing his teeth. The West Indian almost lost his temper. 'Who said that?' The Chinese student shook his head, admitted he didn't know, and went on laughing. 'You didn't go to school, I think you went to the lavatory. Robbie Burns said that. A man is a man for all that, even though he is a louse.' And patting his paper bag shut he went off into the crowd towards the speaker, who was just getting into his stride condemning the Treaty of Versailles.

Portobello Moon

The great delight, of course, of beginning with a title like
that is that nobody has a very clear idea what it means, and
that, according to the theorists at least, it sets the poetic
whisperings going in the reader's mind before he starts
reading the piece itself. To some it could suggest a vague
image of a glowing purple-black waterfront, with loud
yellow lights wriggling in the harbour, and a hint of
impending tragedy in the corruption-scented darkness as
poetically drunken Chinese sailors in the shadows harmo-
nise to a snatch of Kurt Weill. Others might recall a
half-remembered but more brightly-lit picture from some
musical comedy of thirty years ago, with a man in spats
crooning through the rhymes of a complicated lyric against
a line of mauve-lipped chorus girls. And just a few might
gather an impression of gleaming black umbrellas, and the
rain gurgling down the gratings in the Portobello Road.
They could, it is true, hardly be expected to guess that I was
using the word 'moon' in the sense of mournfully
mooching, but then they are by this time, at least according
to the theorists, already hooked.

To those few insomniacs and dental patients, however,
who are still with me, I must admit that this was my original
thought. The Portobello Road, particularly on Saturday
mornings, seems to me to be particularly rich in poetic
ideas: beginning in the bar at Henekeys, where the crowd is
pushing up against the glass partitions by the beer handles
and all talking too loudly because it's Saturday, there's an
odd feeling that everyone is divorced from reality, and yet
at the same time vaguely searching for it in an off-hand sort
of way. It appears at first like a bar full of film extras, with
hairy-looking ginger fur coats, white stockings, black
stockings with suspenders and leg showing, hands wandering about with frayed woollen cuffs and nicotine-stained
dirty finger-nails, wet kisses now and then, and a few dirty

old men sitting and smoking cigarettes with their elbows in puddles of beer just thinking about it.

They all seem divided up, too, like extras on a film set, into Elegant Crowd and Bohemian Crowd, with old public school men, still wearing cavalry-twill trousers and polished brown shoes, lifting their elbows with a sort of saloon-bar self-consciousness and turning their backs on the grimy refugees from Oberammergau drinking behind them. A few isolated clumps of tourists stand staring like visitors to the Zoo who have been asked in for the Chimps' Tea Party.

The same kind of fashionable junk-grubbing goes on at the weekend in Madrid and Paris and Rome, and the tourists have heard that when you're in London this is the place to be on Saturday mornings, especially if you can take in the King's Road earlier on. The sadness of the procession outside is not immediately apparent. There are groups among the crowd who are laughing, and not paying much attention to any of the stalls, just using it as a fashion parade or a place to meet friends. The Happy Wanderers stump through them, marching along at creeping pace in the gutter, banging their big bass drum and making the sound of the saxophone and the trumpet echo back from the modern flats across the road. Occasionally there is a gramophone in a pram or on a stall playing old 78 records, and the honking of cars trying to edge through the crowd. But the whole impression is still one of silent, absent-minded piety reminiscent of a religious celebration in Italy or in Spain, and with the same theatricality and mute nostalgia.

Closer to, where the bored fingers are turning over crucifixes and old rings on the green-baize tables, picking up pieces of chipped china, sorting through fly-blown prints and posters, opening old boxes and cupboards, sorting out beads and rosaries and necklaces, they seem like lost souls, blindly fumbling for some long-lost charm that will suddenly restore them to grace in the eyes of the past. Here in the shops are the ruins of a million homes, dispersed by death, taken apart and out of context, broken toys and glasses and books, now avidly handled by strangers looking for something that might have hung in their grandmother's kitchen if they could only remember what their grandmother's kitchen looked like. Others trying to rebuild the past, trying to furnish their homes with the heirlooms of imaginary ancestors, more attractive than their own. Everything that is old, or even disguised and forged to look old, is believed to have some sacred property, like the relics of the saints, and as the fingers grope on and on, turning over, examining, rummaging among the rusty keys on the table, it seems that their virtue can be received merely by touching them, and that the key of a house that no longer exists can in some mystical way unlock the door to the past and re-establish the owner in the direct tradition and heritage.

It is almost a relief to see the market stalls at the bottom of the hill. After the dreadful army of the dead fumbling among the relics up the hill, the West Indians waiting to buy the oranges and lemons and apples on the fruit barrow seem to stand like a theatrical expression of life and survival.

Lovely Taste

Having received an invitation from a member of the Sainsbury family last week to attend the opening of a new shop in the West End called 'Mr Fish', I had prepared myself for a neon-lit evening among the chromium-rimmed deep freezers and refrigerated slabs, with glasses of cold Chablis and oysters and a hygienic whiff of the sea. There would, I was almost certain, be a great deal of plate-glass, hundreds of square feet of astonishing blue-and-white tiles, a selection of punny slogans based on the words 'sole' and 'plaice', and large mural pictures of smiling codfish standing on their tails in striped aprons, engagingly raising their boaters in greeting

Hence my astonishment at discovering in the dusk just off Bond Street the words 'Mr Fish' in letters of gold above a small square window, artfully lit with spotlights, which cast a jeweller's shop radiance on three shirts of fashionable cut, each with a silk tie knotted at the neck, and suggesting, to the passer-by in the cold street outside, the most exquisite taste and discreet luxury. Indeed, an ecstatic young man pulling on his gloves in the doorway – pushing past a rather gloomy figure with a camera on his shoulder who was trying to force his way in, followed by a mute serf carrying the microphone – summed up the impression made by the window in a single phrase: 'Of course he's always had lovely taste.'

I was almost immediately accosted by a distinguished man in a scarlet coat and white gloves who asked me whether I had an invitation. I only began to realise the sheer hundred-carat quality of the good taste I had presumed to offend, either by my appearance or demeanour, as I looked around me. The walls consisted from floor to ceiling of beautifully polished shelves in some rich rosewood or mahogany, all filled with silken shirt materials, pale yellow, primrose, cinnamon and pink, and lit with discreet little spotlights all the way up. And there, about to leave, was the legendary Twiggy, with very beautiful big grey eyes, and the exact expression of Tweetiepie the Canary recognising Sylvester the Naughty Puddy Tat.

Somewhere in the background, tastefully contemporary music was being played, rather loudly, and the crush, mostly men in narrow-shouldered suits with tiny lapels, ostrich-necked shirts and thick silk ties, was of exactly the right density for the occasion. Glowing with that indefinable glamour that only seems to come out under the skilfully directed spotlights installed by the Interior Decorator, and somehow associated with sweetly spiced after-shave and square-cut hair still warm from the dryer, the guests ground against one another in the tightly jammed crowd, suffering indignities they would not for a moment have tolerated in the theatre or in the Underground with the faintly pained aplomb of the martyr to fashion and, above all, to good taste. A few, it appeared from the gaily swivelling eyes and leaping eyebrows, appeared frankly to enjoy it.

Caught in obstinate eddies in the crowd there were a minority of younger members of the Old Aristocracy, sufficiently faithful to the old conventions to have brought their wives, and a relation of the former Chief Scout was prodding a friend disapprovingly in the chest, flicking open an extravagantly beautiful new shirt: 'Are you wearing a vest under that thing, Henry? How frightfully middle-class.' In other corners, pressed against the shelves, rapturous reunions were taking place among the New Men, reminiscences of long summer afternoons on Italian terraces, and of the even longer titles of those they had spent them with. David Mlinaric, the Interior Decorator, carried his profile past with enviable grace under its cloche of perfectly-set hair, and there was an immediate reaction of wide-eyed excitement. 'Don't you know?' 'That's David Mli . . . Milly . . . Minarick. Anyway, he's one of the Biggest Dandies in London!'

Still struggling, I found myself at last at the bar. Champagne and orange juice seemed to be the most popular drink, and once again I had an opportunity to absorb in relative peace the impeccable good taste of the arrangements. Striped awnings in green and gold hung from rings near the ceiling, and the bar seemed full of adoringly dilated eyes and slowly mouthed compliments. Many of them were directed at a smiling West Indian, his head shaved almost bare, and wearing a beige trouser suit, hairy suede boots to the knee, and a fox fur round the neck. There was also a suspicion of bitchery. 'You know he's basically mouse? Well he is. Anyway, he decided to get it streaked. So he went round to this little place he goes to and he was under the dryer for absolutely hours having each individual streak done and then he came out and do you know what? It was absolutely jet black all over. Promise. Well he was furious, naturally. He had to go back under the dryer and have it all done over again.'

Moving on into the inner sanctum, now decorated for the buffet, the din from the Seeds of Discord, tastefully arranged up on the little catwalk balcony, was deafening. It became impossible, even shouting directly into one's neighbour's ear, to make oneself heard. Again, a few seemed disposed to make a delight out of necessity, and continued to mouth gossip to each other with every display of casual intimacy. The rest of us stood awed and mute, looking up at the rows of perfectly arranged and so far unopened bottles of wine, admired the Harvest Festival splendour of netted cauliflowers, hard-boiled eggs, little rolls of rare roast beef on sticks, freshly fried poppadums and dishes of horseradish, and reflected, unenthusiastic as ever, on the degree of unquestioning, uncritical frenzy that seems to be necessary to realise a personal fantasy and to develop public taste sufficiently to be remembered even as quaint in thirty years' time.

Topless Towers

Still reeling from Christopher Booker's astonishing assault on the mini-skirt in a recent number of the *Weekend Telegraph*, I made my spiritual preparation for the opening of 'La Carretta', the unusual Sicilian restaurant just off Carnaby Street, with considerable care. The invitation was written in discreetly self-effacing English with a slight Italian accent and a suggestion of hunch-shouldered obsequiousness: explaining that 'La Carretta' meant 'The Sicilian Cart', it said that the restaurant had been planned as a rendezvous 'both for the leisurely diner and the businessman-in-a-hurry'. There was a fleeting reference to the possibility of a 'tête-à-tête dinner', and a modest claim that this was London's first Sicilian restaurant and that the dishes would be 'served with a style and a panache never imagined in London before'. But there was no overt reference to the two waitresses whose photographs appeared on the invitation, both wearing what appeared to be sequined backless evening dresses back to front.

The more intriguing of the two photographs, it is true, was described in the text as being 'not just a Sicilian pipe-dream': this showed two suave Italianate business-men, not apparently in a hurry, looking with a kind of shrewd concentration into the almost unnaturally viva-cious eyes of their single lady companion, who was wearing a respectable black dress and showing only a suggestion of shoulder. The unnatural vivaciousness may perhaps have sprung from a desire to compete with the girl standing beside her, seductively sliding a plate of pheasant on to the table with one hand and laying the other, with fingers splayed, on her sequined hip, while her breasts peered, shy and suspicious, slightly to left and right of centre.

Having absorbed as much as possible of the atmosphere from the printed page, I arrived at the romantic little alley where the restaurant is situated a few minutes early in order to avoid being trampled to death. The paved passage is one of those where, anywhere else in Soho, blue-chinned men in luminous blue suits come and breathe in your face and chant, 'Twelve different girls. They're naked and they dance,' in that particular sing-song grimy boredom voice they affect, and where grubby scrubbers lurk in doorways smoking and beckoning lasciviously from the shadows. In Lowndes Court, however, the reception group beneath the light of the doorway was quietly polite, restrained, and suggested rather the sort of group that gathers outside a church hall before a meeting of the church men's club.

Men shifted from one foot to the other, bowed nervously and smiled as they were introduced, and the language seemed to be predominantly Italian. Inside was a roomful of men, all wearing dark suits and talking in low voices under the dim lights, and two tables with cocktail scraps which had already for the most part been eaten. There was a tense atmosphere that was difficult to define, but which was midway between the conspiratorial familiarity of those really breaking the law and the nervously loud heartiness of a rugger club outing to the Folies Bergère. The girl in the cloakroom was quite normally dressed in a little cape and a long dress with a front, and no nudies appeared to have so far arrived.

It became clear that any hope I had of obtaining yet another glittering scoop for the *Spectator* was doomed from the start: most of the men present had thick notebooks and short stubby pencils, both of which they held in tight against their waistcoats as they talked out of the sides of their mouths to waiters and staff. A huge camera and heavy boxes of equipment were being carried in, and there was a good deal of whispering about the BBC news. I therefore settled down to enjoy the mingled emotions of those about to grab the scoop, growing perceptibly impatient now as the promised naked breasts had still not yet been glimpsed.

Looking round at the representatives of the Press it was difficult to believe that any single one of them had never before set at least eyes on a naked breast, and yet it was clear that the excitement of some shared experience, perhaps of the sheer bum-titty-bum vulgarity of it all, was setting a few eyes gleaming more brightly behind thick glasses and stirring up more and more feeling of being at a rugger club party. The Italians slipped in and out of the crowd, sustaining the sense of expectant tension by whispering in each other's ears and looking at their watches, and the Englishmen, Irishmen and Scotsmen reverted more and more to the aggressive camaraderie of the saloon bar, telling dreadful old jokes about the Crucifixion, as if they were consciously hypnotising each other into a state of pagan exultation for the Babylonian Feast to come.

Almost before anyone could point his camera or turn on the television floodlights, the first pair of breasts appeared coming down the stairs. Immediately the roar of pagan incantation was stilled, and the sacred objects were flooded with white light. Cameras whirred, a fat man in a sheepskin jacket pushed backwards into the crowd as they were carried forward, their owner smiling with admirable lack of self-consciousness like a model at a dress show, and there were shouts and instructions about where to hold the tray of goodies she was carrying. The sense of shock seemed to fade with the television lights, and by the time the girl had smiled her way to the other end of the room most of the shouting was over. The next girl stimulated a rather weaker reaction from the crowd: particularly pale of flesh, she seemed uncertain whether the tray should be used as a support or as a shield, and had finally settled for an intermediary position, but so low down that even the most hardened strip-club regulars seemed momentarily baffled by the anatomical problem. There were a few more shouts about safety in numbers, and taking a chance as you only live once, but interest finally shrivelled altogether.

I couldn't help being impressed by the restraint and human consideration of the rugger men in the physical presence of their erotic dream; although few things could have a more anaphrodisiac effect, except perhaps the pieces of cold, pink jelly served on the hors-d'oeuvre tray. I think it was the sight of naked flesh actually working that did it. Perhaps the New Puritans' fears about the shortness of the mini-skirts would be best allayed by leaving them off altogether at work, and insisting on ankle-length bombazine in the evenings.

The Silver Strand

Having prised my disorganised life apart far enough to let in one and a half days of sunlit 'holiday' early last week, I opened a battered 1925 edition of Philips' Handy-Volume *Atlas of the World* at the pages showing Ireland, and ran my finger down the east coast in search of some quiet retreat within easy reach of Dublin. It came to rest on Wicklow. On one side of the black coastline there was the blue of the sea, pale and printed in little dots, with a slightly darker band of blue suggesting placid rollers and gently breaking surf. Inland there was a narrow strip of green, and then pale brown with darker brown hatchings, indicating mountains. The town of Wicklow itself was shown as a little circle, with a firm black curving line linking it to Dublin, three-quarters of an inch farther up the coast. It seemed perfect. Lifting the heavy, old-fashioned, pre-Benn receiver, I dialled the most beautiful girl I had met for the last eight years, the airport, and then retired to bed in a state of suspended disbelief.

Watching the houses distort themselves and flash past in the green bonnet of the monster Rolls-Royce she had discovered somewhere at dawn the next morning, I prepared myself for the usual round of slapstick disasters. But the silver lady swooped on into a cinemascope panorama of glittering blue sky, the Hammersmith overpass snaking towards us over the sunlit housetops at a silent eighty, and Beethoven continuing to boom with concert-hall resonance from a high-fidelity loudspeaker set in the dashboard. Even studying the safety regulations in the booklet 'About your Flight', in which a smiling air-hostess is seen slipping with ice-cool composure into her rubber life-jacket as the aircraft spirals wildly downwards out of control in a trail of oily black smoke, seemed to have no effect: the sun flashed and vibrated on the engine casings and we remained suspended in the crystal-blue sky over the deep-blue Irish Sea. I even relaxed sufficiently to begin drawing sea-monsters on the BEA maps without political significance provided for the convenience of travellers.

At Dublin airport, the taxi driver had the weatherbeaten face of an Irish bit-part actor, with thick white hair, stout bronzed forearms and an almost unnaturally authentic Irish accent. 'The planes have been landing there this morning in all shapes and forms and sizes. A man said it was on account of them opening a new cathedral in Dublin. That's ridiculous. The last time they said they were going to open a new cathedral was back in 1934. They found a site for it and put up a sign saying that was where they were going to build it. Twenty years went by and nothing happened. Then they took the sign down.' The old car was driven recklessly, with abandoned thrusts on the accelerator, always on collision course with the bonnets of oncoming buses, and then swerving at the last moment either to the left or the right of them as it took the driver's fancy. Finally, we rolled on to the pavement outside Trinity College.

From then on I accepted the fact that I was the victim of some elaborate fairy masque put on by the Irish Tourist Board. The Book of Kells was there, beautifully painted in purples and yellows and reds on the 1200-year-old vellum, set out in its glass case under the dim wooden barrel vaulting of the library; outside there were plump little gipsy beggar-girls in the back streets, pulling at your arm and asking for something to get a bite to eat 'and I'll pray for you'. There was even a ludicrous old woman standing on the pavement with a full-size harp, grappling with it as if with an awkward chest-expander, and producing random and uncoordinated plunks apparently without thought of financial gain. We ended up in an authentic Irish pub called the 'Old Stand', full of the rich murmur of good conversation and Irish wit.

On the way down to Wicklow the mountains flashed green and gold through the trees, German schools lay back from the road among the rhododendrons, and a small but poetic group of gipsy ponies and two caravans stood waiting in a grass lay-by. The town, when we got there, was dusty and grey in the hot sunlight, with narrow pavements and little shops selling brightly painted leprechauns and ashtrays with little homilies and sayings written on them. In the dining-room of the Grand Hotel, full of little tables and waitresses in black with white aprons, there was a contented Irish family, an elderly father and mother and their daughter, who was a nun, and their son, sitting opposite her, a priest: in profile they had the red, simply drawn faces of those watching miracles in primitive religious paintings. The roast beef was excellent, the wine was fragrant and gently intoxicating and must have been there for years and years, and in the placid, timeless atmosphere the conversation wandered lovingly over the flesh, the spirit, and the nature of God.

'If you want a good walk,' they said, 'you should go to the Silver Strand. It's two miles by the road, but it's more beautiful over the cliffs.' The lane out of the town, with freshly painted park seats in pale blue and canary yellow, was full of Irish children chasing each other with sticks and shouting, but out along the cliffs there was no sound but the warm wind and the surf foaming round the wet rocks. Gulls perched, hunching their shoulders, on the white-splashed grey stone ledges at the clifftop, and then took off as we came closer, wheeling away into the wind and squealing; sheep that had been lying against the rock outcrops in the sun got up and trotted knobble-kneed up the hill, twitching their tails: if there had been another soul in sight it would have seemed like a cigarette commercial. All the time the sun got hotter and hotter, and we pushed waist-high through the bracken, and then up through a hot cleft in the rocks where the seed-grass came away in dry, dusty handfuls, and where we could see all along the coast to the Silver Strand. It looked miles and miles away, so we stopped on Wicklow Head by the old stone tower, and looked across at the lighthouse opposite, with an old lady sitting at the foot of it and knitting. I think she might even have been wearing a shawl. The Tourist Board are devils for detail.

Omens at the Fair

From the crumbling off-yellow sand at the seashore, littered with sodden egg-boxes and crisp packets, the seaside town of Seaton Carew, on the bay between West Hartlepool and Middlesbrough, looked subtly beautiful last Sunday afternoon. There was a whiff of chlorine in the wind from the ICI works over the horizon at Billington, the sea that came hissing up the sand was slate-black, and away beyond the town the chimneys of the South Durham Iron and Steel Works smoked silver-white into a dove-grey sky. The houses facing the sea had the vertical simplicity of illustrations in a children's story book, some of them painted pink and some blue. In the foreground dark figures stood about fully clothed in the stilted attitudes of holidaymakers in old seaside photographs, and at the end of the flat promenade the yellow framework of a Big Dipper and the slender spokes of a red and yellow Ferris Wheel rose about the corrugated-iron fence round the Fun Fair. Near us on the beach an old man in a dark blue pin-stripe double-breasted suit with very wide shoulders and a flat cloth cap stood lopsidedly with his hands behind his back, watching it all.

As we kicked our way closer across the powdery sand, the rattle of the ratchet on the Big Dipper became audible against the amplified twanging of guitars, and we watched the little red-painted car being drawn at snail's pace up the forty-five-degree incline to roll rumbling round the iron curves, down the mechanical slope, and up the other side. One party of six adults managed a feeble scream of pleasure as the car plunged downwards, but most of them rushed down the dip in sophisticated silence. The fairground was shabby inside and floored with rough asphalt. The slowly drifting crowd was predominantly young: there were teenage girls with their hair chopped short and dark stockings, some of them dancing in twos and threes in corners to the deafening beat of the music – the confused cacophony of other fairgrounds had been reduced here to the pillar-shaking din of a single loudspeaker system – boys in check trousers and windcheaters leaning against the railings round the Bumper Cars, a few older parents with little fat boys in double-breasted jackets and matching shorts with white ankle socks. A baby with unusually large and lustrous brown eyes leant back on its mother's breast, pointing with one finger like an Infant Christ in an Adoration of the Magi, and silently mouthed the word 'Bow-wow'.

The bow-wow in question was a sandy-haired Alsatian, a mean-looking dog held back on a short black leash by a policeman in a sharply-raked peak cap. Other children who toddled up to pat it drew back screaming with their hands over their faces as it gave a white-toothed snarl and tried to spring forward, dragged back finally by its handler. As I looked more closely at the crowd I became aware of more policemen, all standing solitary and watchful, ignored by the pleasure-seekers.

Sensing some dim Bergmanesque symbolism in the emergence of these tight-lipped black angels of death and determinism into the bright pageant of life, I resolved to abandon the role of cynical bystander immediately and to step into the bright pageant before it was too late.

The two little girls who had suggested the fair in the first place said we should go on the chair-o-planes. I clambered into the rusty bucket-seat that hung twisting on four thin chains, concealed my misgivings and assumed a bland smile. The chains on which we depended appeared to be ancient, rusty and fragile: the trajectory we swung out on as the tower began to turn passed perilously close to the roofs of nearby booths – a white painted sign saying 'Hot Water and Jugs of Tea' and 'Drink Hubbly Bubbly' whirled past inches away with increasing frequency and momentum – and soon the thickly-peopled earth began to lurch sickly and heavily beneath us, the whole horizon at one stage appearing to tip and wobble. With the asphalt still unsteady beneath my feet, I allowed myself to be led by an infant hand to an appalling device called The Caterpillar. Trapped underneath a canvas hood, we sat in pathetic silence among the childish laughter and squeals of delight, flung up and down, thrown against the outer side of the little train, rattled and jolted over the rollers. Assisted down the steps, I was just about to re-affirm the validity of cynical bystanding as against painful commitment when it was suggested that I should visit the Lady Palmist.

I had been warned that the Lady Palmist in question tended to see the future mainly in terms of Men in Uniform, Large Buildings in which one went to sign important documents, and assistance from Middle-Aged Men. Nevertheless, considering the policemen still standing silent in the crowd, I felt doomed finally to face up to the mysterious powers of limiting destiny and judgment. As a last defence, I assumed a thick French accent, entered the booth, which contained a sofa, an upright chair, a bare table, and bade the Lady Palmist a good afternoon. She placed a small glass ball on the palm of my left hand and told me that she could see a water-crossing ahead. I raised my eyebrows in gallic surprise. She also saw a man in uniform, perhaps from across the water. Then she saw a large building into which I should have to go to sign an important document. That, she replied in answer to my hesitant question, might be across the water too. I could also expect help from a middle-aged man. I asked if he was French. She said she didn't think so, but he had travelled a lot abroad. I thanked her and asked her how she knew all this. She looked at me narrowly with her extraordinarily perceptive grey eyes, and replied, 'It's a gift, dear.'

Attic Farce

Doomed by the Lady Palmist of Seaton Carew to cross the water, I found myself last Tuesday evening on the time-worn steps of the Acropolis. The air was heavy and still full of heat, and the sun was going down like beaten gold in a rose-purple haze beyond Piraeus: a few people were standing about or squatting on rocks, talking quietly in French or German or American – 'But it has such *per*fect per*por*tions. You know, I have simply fallen in love with Greece, George' – and down beneath us the city was turning to a warm sandstone glow as the light left it. Looking up towards the Parthenon, still dominant in sun-yellow stone against the blue-green evening sky, I was just about to go through the little iron gate and wander poetically over the still-warm flagstones, indulging in inaccurate musings on the ancient past, when a brown hand was laid on my arm.

The man was wearing a peaked cap and had a neatly-clipped black moustache. He waved his hand wearily over the sunset: 'Is dust.' I looked back towards the sea. 'No, is cloase. Ferme. Is sut.' I then saw a notice saying that the gates were closed at dusk, regretted my frail grasp of Greek and familiar chronic disorganisation, thanked him and began to walk back down the hill again. I followed a narrow and dusty path leading down under the olive trees, with little mushroom-shaped green metal lamps and the soft screeching of crickets, and came out in front of the Herodes Atticus Theatre, a semi-ruinous building at the foot of the hill. The gold disc of the sun had now broken in half in the west, and the light was fading fast. A tall, stooping American in a blue jacket was buying tickets at a little window in the wall, and, having nothing better to do, I followed his example. I later discovered that I had bought a seat for the Bucharest Opera Ballet's performance of *Swan Lake*.

I arrived at the theatre just as the last gong was sounded

and the lights went down in the steep arena. The entrance being beside the stage, I had to brush past the chorus who were sitting along the edge of it, the men dressed in skull-caps and white beards, the women in nuns' head-dresses, and all wearing long costumes of faded blue and black. The effect, as they sat motionless, looking straight out in front of them, and lit from below by the lights of the orchestra pit, was strikingly dramatic, and, it occurred to me as I climbed up with other latecomers to the back of the theatre, strangely Greek in mood for a production of *Swan Lake*, even by the Bucharest Opera Ballet. Also, the music of the overture, played by a large orchestra in the semi-circular area in front of the stage, seemed a little modern and discordant for Tchaikovsky. The lights came up on the stage to reveal a number of girls in flimsy white muslin costumes, with silver bands in their hair, dancing about in front of a King and Queen on thrones, apparently celebrating some form of religious rite.

This dance continued for some time, interspersed with harsh choral comments from the seated choristers. After this, a number of frankly effeminate men in white mini-skirts and in various stages of sunburn came prancing in, their leader attempting to mime colourfully to a flute being played in the orchestra. An elderly sage, in floor-length white garments and a lustrous beard, was then led on by what was either a very elderly child or an operatic dwarf, and sang various remarks of such obvious offensiveness – I was uncertain what language they were singing in: I assume it was Rumanian, but it could equally well at times have been Yiddish or Norman French – that the King, a man with fat legs in a red cloak, fell to the ground with exaggerated gestures of horror, and all the virgins extinguished their antique torches with a series of uncoordinated clicks.

The second act found the King alone in a dark landscape, with a single papier-mâché rock and a lit cloud-effect moving over the ruined wall that forms the back of the amphitheatre. Lightning flickered at the broken stone windows, and three men rushed on to the stage. The King faced them, sang one note, and then flung himself upon them, bopping each of them with a blow from his rather flimsy club in a series of heavy balletic sweeps, and then fled from the stage. A servant ran in, stooped over the bodies, sang the word 'mort', or it could have been 'mord', and then hurried away into the wings, his sandals creaking on the canvas-covered floor. My mystification was complete when two men in black trousers and black shirts came on to move the papier-mâché rock and revealed the King, looking if anything fatter than before, singing in a high falsetto voice. It was some moments before I realised that the King was merely listening energetically, and that the voice itself came from one of the ladies of the chorus.

During the interval I bought a programme. *Swan Lake* had been the night before. What I had been watching was *Oedipus Rex*, by Enesco. I returned to another seat, higher up in the marble-faced and rather hard arena, humbled at my ignorance, and marvelling at the genius of the geometrician who thought of so simple an idea for seating 5,000 people in such a small space and all so close to the stage. I decided to concentrate on enjoying the second half for itself alone. Almost immediately the lights on the music stands in the orchestra pit went out. The blind soothsayer, caught in mid-aria, peered into the darkness, but was unable to see the conductor, and the performance stopped, leaving the cast leaning on their spears in attitudes of bashful ennui. When a man in a white shirt had finally struggled through the close-packed musicians, pushed a harp out of the way, and mended the fault, I was completely on their side, and for the rest of the evening, with the corner of the Parthenon high above us on one side, and a white moon rising over Athens on the other, I accepted it all, including the music, as beautiful, even when right at the end they festooned Oedipus's corpse with a huge chocolate-box bow of white muslin. I'm sure the Ancient Greeks would have done it that way.

Over the Sea to Seriphos

Wishing to visit friends on the island of Seriphos in the Cyclades, I went last week to the offices of Thos. Cook and Sons in Athens. The man behind the counter listened gloomily, pulling at his moustache in a manner suggesting black despair. It was, he explained, impossible to buy steamer tickets in Athens, and I would have to go to Piraeus, some five miles away. I thanked him, and crossed the road to the agency opposite, where I was immediately provided with a ticket by a smiling obsequious infant of twelve, who also gave me a neatly printed timetable in which the shipping routes to the islands were set out in black and white. The timetable was issued by Hermes, traditionally, among other things, the Conductor of Souls, and I left the agency secure in a naïve pagan optimism.

I arrived at the docks at nine next morning, an hour before the *Pandelis* was due to leave. The boat had not come in yet, and I was directed to a quiet gathering of Greeks sitting among their baggage on the quayside. It was already very hot, policemen in white were blowing their whistles and shouting at drivers, and the heavily-laden lorries banged and rumbled up the steel ramps. An old biscuit-seller, with one hand and a rather distressing divided stump, came and sat beside me on my suitcase and began sorting out his basket. It all seemed a colourful background to my reading on the Russian Revolution, and I settled down contentedly with Isaac Deutscher. At half-past ten I walked over to the shipping office, and was told that the boat had been delayed: it would be in now at half-past eleven. Returning to the other refugees on the quay, I became immersed in my book once again, and finally went back to the shipping office at half-past twelve. The man affected polite curiosity. I reminded him of our former conversation. He shrugged and looked at the ceiling. There was no boat. Tomorrow. Not today.

It was in this way that I found myself sitting on the deck of the *Myrtidiotissa* an hour or so later, eating a huge half-moon of water-melon with a very old and toothless lady in black, with the wind fluttering in the awning above and the white spray drifting away from the bows across the swimming-pool blue sea, bound for Syros. The island is about twenty miles from Seriphos, and the man at the office said I might be able to get a boat across. Examining the timetable more closely, it seemed more likely that I might not, so I decided to abandon Seriphos for the moment, and go down to Santorini, dramatically described to me before I left by Sean Kenny as 'this great black wall rising up out of the sea with the little white houses right up at the top of the cliff.' I arrived in Syros, compared my timetable with the painted noticeboard outside the harbour office to confirm that there was a steamer leaving for Santorini the next evening at seven, and sat down to enjoy a simple but intoxicating supper beside the gently-lapping black waters of the harbour.

When I came back the following evening, the clerk could hardly have been more helpful. Taking my timetable, he examined it in silence for three or four minutes, then took a soft lead pencil and crossed out the word Syros against the date in question. The boat did not call there any more. There was, however, a boat leaving for Mykonos in half an hour. I went gratefully aboard, and leant on the rail filled with a sense of purpose and progress as the ship churned on through the dimly foaming water under the bright stars. The lights of the island grew more distinct, and eventually the anchor clanked out and splashed into the harbour. I turned to an affable old sailor to reassure myself that this was Mykonos. He said it was indeed, and wished me an agreeable stay. It was not until the ship had sailed that I found out purely by chance that it was in fact Tinos.

After a peaceful cruise in a small boat to Delos and Mykonos, I returned to Tinos to ask about boats to Santorini. The clerk was bright but firm. There were no boats going to Santorini. There was a boat for Santorini leaving the next evening at seven from Syros, but the boat to Syros from Tinos did not arrive until after it had gone. Smugly believing that I could break the system, I went next door to the office of a rival line. A domestic scene was in progress, the small plump wife weeping quietly in a corner and the husband tapping his fingers angrily on the desk. He brightened at my approach. He said there was of course a boat to Syros, at eight in the morning. While buying the ticket, I mentioned *en passant* that I had been afraid of missing the boat for Santorini in the evening. He looked at me suspiciously. The next boat to Santorini from Syros was in three days' time. I drew his attention to the timetable. He dismissed it, growing angry again. His wife, smiling at me encouragingly through her tears, said quietly that perhaps there was a boat from another line. This drove him mad. Getting down off his high stool, he walked purposefully across the room and slapped her.

Some days later, after an idyllic and fruitful time in Santorini wandering among the ruins of ancient Thyra high above the sea, where a guide came running fifty yards through the rubble, waving his arms in order to show me a phallic symbol carved on a broken wall, and down among the smoking ovens of bright yellow sulphur in the crater of the volcano, I rode down the cliff path in the darkness on the bony back of an elderly mule to the harbour in order to take the night boat back to Athens and from there to Seriphos. I entered the harbour-master's office and asked whether the Athens boat had been delayed. He shrugged and repeated the gesture of looking at the ceiling. There were no boats tonight. I thanked him, and went out to sit on the quay, wondering whose nerve would snap first. After an hour he came out. He apologised. There was a boat, yes. It would dock in half an hour. Still glowing with overweening confidence that I had finally beaten the gods, I climbed the unsteady gangway and was shown into my cabin. The next morning I asked the steward when we would be arriving at Piraeus. He said he did not know. We should, however, be in Rhodes about midnight. Next year I am going to sacrifice a goat to Hermes before I start.

Crushing Yokes

Fancy Free

Being a bachelor, I stress, whatever image of sulky, kohl-rimmed eyes and high-uplift buttocks in pink needle-cord churning mesmerically along in the twilight of the Old King's Road the word may conjure up in the contemporary mind, is the very essence of masculinity. Light and sprightly, Samson before Delilah got the shears out, ready on a roll of drums to explode Houdini-like out of the chains and padlocks of any emotional entanglement and land graceful and poised to a touch on the cymbals, ready for fresh feats, bright-eyed and unencumbered: he travels fastest who travels alone.

He may ultimately, to quote whatever fop in a curly wig and frilly furbelows said it in the first place, by degrees dwindle into a husband, but as a practising bachelor he is God before the Creation, Michelangelo up the ladder with a dripping brush and a bare ceiling, Man before the Fall, enjoying the Golden Age of the Imagination before the miseries of commitment.

Not so Big Doris in the Typing Pool. She has plumped, as they say in the restaurant reviews, for the most expensive thing on the menu.

The bachelor feels pain, somewhere long ago and far away, like a patient under the anaesthetic vaguely aware that an extraction has occurred. Because the restaurant, the bachelor's natural habitat, is the place where he has come to escape that kind of thing. Here he is, leather-bound menu open in front of him, a familiar prop in his Sophisticated Perusal act, eyebrows half lifted, eyes being dragged back like dogs on the leash from looking at the right-hand column where the prices are: Lugosi the Head

Waiter hangs hunched like a question-mark, pencil licked over his order-pad, his mobile face turned aside to semaphore a welcome of fiendish intensity to the well-dressed couple at the door. The bachelor could not be in a more characteristic and contented attitude: the choice unmade, every possibility left open, lips pursed, about to ask how the quails are tonight, and Big Doris has taken the high dive into the caviar.

The bachelor is not entirely certain that he likes Big Doris anyway. Were he in the position of his married friends, sitting down at this moment to a nourishing supper at one tenth the cost of Big Doris's main course without the vegetables, he would probably have settled for half an hour of *Charlie's Angels* and the News. Then after lunch Big Doris reached out for the Tippex, the lift of a breast in a sweater, and here we are. There is also something wrong about supper assembled out of familiar cupboards, however easily, between the evening paper and bathing the baby or between one nervous breakdown and the next, inevitable and too much like real life.

For the Prospero and sole inhabitant of his heterosexual fairy-land, the bachelor's dinner has to materialise, like the cloud-capp'd towers and indeed the great Globe itself, by magic. No squabbles with Big Doris or anybody else about who Brillo-pads the burnt saucepan, no guilt, no crinkly fingers, so the restaurant.

This is after all the prelude to the bachelor's greatest unpainted ceiling of all, the wide-screen extravaganza in teeth-jarring Sensurround, in which Big Doris falls a victim to the Thousand Loving Thrusts, the Congress of the Mad Gorilla, or whatever else the Manual may recommend for afterwards. Admittedly the first time Doris said she wasn't feeling very well and thought she ought to have an early night, and on the last occasion her mother was staying. No matter. No grim edge of reality must be allowed to protrude in this opening movement of the fantasia, the heady gastronomic helter-skelter ride that will unlock the gentle floodgates of lust, even in Big Doris. The bachelor, like God before the Creation, is an optimist.

Lugosi takes the order, and after various patronising enquiries from the bachelor about Lugosi's wife and children, clicks his heels, inclines his head with a little knowing turn of the chin, and vanishes.

Patronising is the key word. There is only one *patron*, in the bachelor's scheme of things, who *mange ici*. Every night of the year, in some dream-palace or another: paying single-handed for the roof to be rebuilt, for Lugosi to perform as Court Chamberlain, for what his bank-manager would recognise, in terms of personal economics, as a three-dimensional fiction.

Few women, oddly enough, going to a restaurant of their own accord, would dream of treating Lugosi – a man who by daylight no one would risk having in the house even to read the gas-meter – like a long-lost friend, or going through the grisly old charade with the wine-list: but then few women are to be found dressing up in dirty macs to cluster round the Explicit Films Books and Mags. Men are the masters when it comes to works of the imagination – witness Beethoven, Bach etcetera – and the imagination from time to time needs shoring up. Hence the insane expense of the restaurant, where the bachelor for a brief moment every night can be acknowledged Lord of the Manor.

Admittedly the decor may not be exactly what he would choose for his own dining room, which he could build three times over for the money he spends in a year: admittedly the company he finds there, even overlooking Lugosi and his band of two-faced thieves, is of the kind he would, in his right mind, pay good money to avoid sharing a taxi with, let alone eat with. And Big Doris is about to break the news about her boy-friend arriving on the eleven-ten from Inverness.

Standing on the pavement, with all the glory gone, can it ever occur to him that somewhere in a darkened bedroom, mere mounds under the bedclothes, his married friends, the fortunate fools, are fast asleep? And that it might be time, even for Prospero, to break his magic wand and get down to a bit of serious Dwindling?

Slaving Away

I am sharply aware, in setting down these brief impressions of my week as a housewife, that the ground had been trampled fairly flat by numerous other victims, willing and unwilling, of the so-called Sexual Revolution.

Some comment has been intentionally humorous: there was for instance a series of drawings by Larry some years ago under the general title 'Man in Apron', in which a lugubrious and resigned husband was seen, in one instance, bringing in the washing as it came on to rain with a brassiere knotted under his chin to keep his ears dry.

Much of the rest has been unintentionally so: James – now Jan – Morris, a person of sterner stuff when it came to long-term commitment, described the rapture, after his/her Operation, of being whistled at by his/her first taxi-driver and then given a boisterous kiss on both cheeks: an extra that may, for all I know, be thrown in for every middle-aged lady passenger in these days of economic recession in the cab trade, but which convinced the former Mr Morris that she had triumphantly arrived, like Christian in *Pilgrim's Progress*, on the Other Side.

The purpose of this exercise however being only exploratory, I shall do my best to stick to the kind of brief notes made by potholers, travellers to strange parts, and otherwise virtuous dons at Oxford who have experimented with hallucinatory drugs. I have also avoided any topic which might be deemed rude, like laundry.

The seven-day trial took place in Tewkesbury, where my companion and I had rented a cottage with a view of the Abbey and fully equipped with everything except towels and bedlinen.

It was agreed that the swap was to be one-way. She was in the terminal stages of revision for A-level English, preparatory to entering London University as a mature student, which prevented her from taking over my work as a Creative Artist – falling through the ceiling for beer commercials, collaborating on humorous columns in satirical magazines, teaching, discussing illusory projects over all-too-solid lunches, and grinding away at the various bits of writing and performing – that would under normal circumstances have occupied my week. I also, out of respect for the good burghers of Tewkesbury and the fragile seams of my companion's wardrobe, plumped, as they say in restaurant columns, for wearing my own clothes.

Rising

For the Creative Artist, everything can be put down, in terms of squaring accounts with one's conscience, as 'work'.

This includes lying half-asleep and letting the first incisive pattern of bird song or the gentle murmur and surge of traffic infiltrate the consciousness with the smell of coffee and frying bacon, postponing any summons to the spreadeagled extremities until the call of 'Breakfast's ready', and sometimes a good deal longer. Each stage of brightening awareness might one day be refined – or so the Creative Artist argues – into some golden moment of theatre, second of celluloid, or purple passage on the page.

Getting up first and cooking the breakfast hasn't got the same sense of repose or receptive awareness, but it does give one the political edge.

Dishwashing

Part of the excitement of being a full-time Creative Artist is that everything has to be new, or so the theory goes. However long the run of a play, however tedious the book to be reviewed, however old the joke, every performance, every line, every new twist to the gag must, like each new human face hurled by the Creator from the void, be different. The same cannot be said of washing-up.

There may be a certain craftsmanlike satisfaction in scraping the last bit of dried egg yolk off the spoon and there is even something approaching artistic satisfaction in soaking a wine-glass in hot water and polishing it to a gleam with a clean dry cloth. But shutting the cutlery drawer on a bunch of knives and forks that are, at best, only as good as before you started eating with them does not measure up to stamping one's unique personality in the eternal granite.

Bedmaking

There are nevertheless moments in the life of the Creative Artist when the need to be original in itself becomes a burden. Better an unambitious job, capable of satisfactory completion. Hence the consolation of bed-making.

There is of course a paradox: it should logically be as boring as doing the spoons; but making a bed you are at least making something that didn't exist when you began, and there is some soothing security in the lingering animal warmth, the contrasting texture of sheets and blankets, the traditional theatrical activity of plumping pillows (Comic Maid Act I Scene I swapping exposition with the Butler), and even a simple-minded delight in symmetry. Whatever the case, bedmaking is almost bearable for a week, even solo and having to go round the other side to pull the top sheet straight; performed as a joint activity it is actually tolerable, perhaps even the basis for some sort of sacramental habit.

Dusting

Dust, which golden boys and girls all must come to, seems to me a more terrible *memento mori* than any skull on the desk or empty coffin standing open in the corner of the study.

The idea of slow flakes of decay falling invisibly for all eternity, making a mockery of seven maids with seven mops or any other human endeavour to clear them up, is as terrifying as any science fiction horror yet conceived. The Creative Artist prefers not to think about such things, except for large sums of money or when, as above, he is making a morbid meal of it. He lives, as is observable at any lunch where a Creative Writer is trying to obtain money from a producer or publisher, in a paradise of perfect ideas, eternal, incorruptible, and only rarely dragged into the real world with more than a shred of their excellence intact.

Yet there is the lone, heroic housewife, always on duty in

the front line of reality, fighting the losing battle day after day after day. I was so upset I couldn't even get the Hoover out.

Shopping

Selection, as any manual of Creative Art will tell you, is central to the Creative Process. The hues you choose, as the late Godfrey Winn used to sing, the pinks and blues, when you paint from the palette of love. Going to the shops is a good deal more nerve-racking.

There is, certainly, the awe experienced by the economist Manderville in the early years of the eighteenth century, as he cut open a newly imported pineapple and smelt the juice on his fingers, at the wonder of world trade; Tewkesbury's celery, in the vegetable-scented greengrocer's where the other housewives and I waited our democratic turn, comes from France, her oranges from Israel and her lettuce from California. But the wonder of world trade is soon eclipsed by the mysteries of local commerce. Contrary to all economic theory, the little old lady who runs a tiny general shop opposite the Abbey, by dint of haggling with the vanman, is able to sell the oranges for fivepence less than the supermarkets or the big greengrocers at the other end of the town. Hence a time-wasting maze to be threaded through Tewkesbury's ancient streets and muddy riverside alleys, trying to hold a steady course from shop to shop against the pull of siren voices promising tuppence off.

More misleading still, to the heavy-laden Creative Artist – having unwisely chosen the wine merchants as first port of call – the final picture for which you are selecting the elements is not as luminously present in the mind as was, let us say, the *Laughing Cavalier* to Frans Hals before he first dipped his brush in the turps. The thematic connection between a tin of Explosive Curried Beef Risotto Surprise and a roll of lavatory paper may by blindingly obvious to the experienced housewife, living as she does in the real world of gurgling bowels and ever-falling dust, in touch with the everlasting grind of the machinery of matter.

Not so to the Creative Artist, part-time lavatory humorist though he may be.

Cooking

D. H. Lawrence, we are told, got into a terrible temper when he opened the lid of a piano for the first time in his life and was unable to play the Moonlight Sonata. I felt the same frustration when left alone with a gas stove. Watching a sausage beginning to brown or scrambled eggs thickening, I glimpsed the far-off Everest of Cooking as Creative Art, but pots and plates accumulated in the sink and things tended to catch fire.

My thoughts, like the toast, turned to blacker things. I became cynically, though by no means unhappily, aware of the utterly stupid boring repetitive pointlessness of the back-stage side of eating, if, like D. H. Lawrence, you are banned by inexperience from the creative paradise of Monsieur Champignon the Chef.

The digestive process itself became a terrible metaphor. French celery ripped out of the ground, Israeli oranges torn from the trees, Californian lettuces plucked up, peacefully grazing cattle in the Argentine struck down and pulped in colourfully labelled tins of Explosive Risotto, all to be gathered together in cardboard boxes with the other cans and packets and rolls of lavatory paper, sucked in through the front door, forcing the housewife through a series of physical jerks as automatic as the contractions of the large intestine, and finally evacuated through the back door and into the dustbin.

Conclusions

I have not covered the question of children, since none were involved in the test, but bearing in mind their emotional and practical demands, gnawing away at the housewife's identity and personal possessions with the grisly efficiency of caterpillars stripping a cabbage leaf, I was left with the same dumb admiration you feel for the heroes of Samuel Beckett, far away from the comforting dreams in the firelight, up against the dark. All the times I've ever offered to dry up seem now like the most hypocritical kind of Uncle Tomism. Next time I set off to go and roll round laughing for a couple of hours, I may describe it as 'work', but I shall try not to.

The End

The Good Old Days

From The Wilsonian Idyll, *by Angus Windsor-Frost Junior, to be published in the early part of 2069 by Weidenfeld and Weidenfeld at N£55.*

Looking back at the late sixties of the last century, lost now, alas, for ever and melted away in the corrosive acid that is time past, we cherish what is inevitably a nostalgic and idealised image of a Golden Age, an Elysium where it was always midsummer, and where the air was for ever alive with music, laughter and the warbling of songbirds. How we love to imagine the People's Harold himself, his spry, portly figure swathed in an austere lounge suit of the period, strolling informally perhaps in the Park of St James's on the arm of Mr Brown, bowing now and then to a 'mini-skirted' acquaintance, as the colourful old Zodiacs and Zephyrs glided past along the Mall and a lilting air of Lennon and McCartney's drifted across the grass that still grew there in profusion, from some antique Japanese 'portable'!

To a cultivated man living in England in the second half of the twentieth century, life must indeed have seemed idyllic. Poised for a fragile moment between the rough disciplines of man's primitive state and the effete anarchy into which he was so soon to decline, twentieth-century bourgeois society could feel confident as never before. Surrounded on the one hand by the jealously preserved traditions of a conservative civilisation, and on the other by the miraculous innovations of an advanced technology, the Wilsonians could congratulate themselves on achieving in their lifetime that blessed state so often alluded to by their

222

own visionary Harold, the earthly paradise. They could still wander, as their forefathers had done, through the 'fields' at harvest time, or watch the cattle grazing at liberty among the picturesque ruins of some ancient abbey, and yet they could, if they so pleased, flash in perfect comfort through the upper air to exchange such rustic scenes for the jagged palm fronds and hissing surf of a tropical island. Once there, they could sprawl on the sand, without protective clothing, and look up as the gentle darkness fell, at a moon already girdled with artificial satellites.

And of all the Elysian Fields, England could surely at this time have laid claim to being among the most desirable. Educated and enlightened by the recently invented television – and it is hard for us today to imagine the purity and inspiration of the medium at that time of its pristine innocence – travellers from all over the planet flocked to these islands to see for themselves the riches of an ancient culture, displayed in surroundings of exquisite taste. Of the architectural glories of the City, of seaside resorts like Brighton, Southend or Bognor Regis we have today only the dimmest inkling from the work of archaeologists and the few pieces of documentary evidence that have survived the events of the intervening years. Reading those speeches of the Wilson Ministry that have come down to us, however, it must be obvious that the New Jerusalem of which they spoke was no idle metaphor. Wide 'streets', open to the sky, along which it was possible to walk or to travel in a private motor-car without the sound of gunfire or danger of any kind: large tracts of unpolluted water which must closely have resembled the 'rivers' of earlier times: and, when no natural cloud obscured the sun, a brilliant blue sky above, sometimes entirely silent for minutes on end, and innocent altogether of space rattle or re-entry megabooms.

For a twentieth-century 'family' – the smallest social unit, still based on natural coupling and reproduction – life would begin each day very much as it had for their primitive ancestors. Such night lighting as there was in no way dispelled the darkness as it does today, and the first streaks of sunlight appeared in the east, filtered and distorted through a still existent atmosphere to produce exotic colourings of pink and yellow behind the fantastic natural shapes formed by the clouds of water vapour. After a simple meal of traditional foods, still for the most part produced by traditional agricultural methods, the male would leave 'home' – consisting in those days in some cases of as much as two large 'rooms' for as few as five or six ciphers, privately decorated and furnished – and set off through the open air without any kind of breathing apparatus for his place of 'work'.

Even though this activity, as some commentators have suggested, may well have become ritualised by the late twentieth century, it nevertheless represented the continuance of an ancient tradition, formed a basis at least for the economic and social order, and provided the mature male with a source of pride and self-esteem compensated for today only by drugs and psychological intervention. Nor did this activity occupy more than a part of the male life-cycle. What evidence we have suggests that at times set aside for the consumption of natural food social contacts of a highly sophisticated nature were established, and that in the evening – a time of day when the light very gradually left the atmosphere, once again creating what must have been inconceivably beautiful effects in the sky – there was opportunity for public entertainment or for private diversion.

Apart from the 'holidays' I alluded to earlier, when twentieth-century man was permitted apparently to pass freely from one state to another purely in the pursuit of pleasure, a central element in his life appears to have been an almost obsessive interest in the displays and rituals culminating in the satisfaction of the primitive sexual instincts. To this obsession, which might seem to us today comic were our own lot not so tragic, much of his artistic and scientific ingenuity was sacrificed. The naïve pleasure he took in it must if anything increase our envy of him at that epoch, freed at last by advances in science to couple at will and without responsibility, and still able to enjoy to the full the mounting sense of sensual delight and cathartic climax so graphically described in Fragment C, brought to light during the excavation of the glazed-tile boundary wall of the Whitehall Palace.

And yet, we must ask ourselves, piecing together with tweezers the few charred fragments we have of Wilsonian Papers found in the Palace, and listening to those weird voices and fleeting faces still preserved on a few inches of 'video-tape' discovered in the radioactive pools towards the western limit of the original site of London, could a doubt ever have crossed their minds as they strolled beneath those leafy trees, under a blue sky that might at worst threaten pure rain? For their sakes we must hope that it did not.

HOW TO AVOID FLYING
by Cliff Parker

Afeared of flying? If so, remember that statistics prove that forty-seven times more people die of old age in airport departure lounges than are hurt in crashes. Yet unbelievably, airlines only demonstrate survival techniques to the few who actually get on a plane.

This book, then, is your survival kit for use during those long bleak days and nights, waiting for take off.

Just settle in with your week's supply of packed lunches among the rows of untenanted car rental booths and banks closed till tomorrow, and read.

Don't worry about the flight. It will probably never happen. Scheduled or charter, if it's going to somewhere desirable it will be cancelled due to air traffic controllers/baggage handlers/cabin staff strikes. The only ones that actually get away are those going to places like Abu Dhabi that no one in their right mind would want to go to anyway.

When you've finished the book you can go home, refreshed, happy and safe.

NEW ENGLISH LIBRARY

THE CATS' GUIDE TO PEOPLE
by Stewart Cowley

Any cat who has chosen to adopt humans will confirm that they are a welter of contradictions; temperamental yet predictable, self-centred yet loyal, arrogant yet vulnerable, and very often neurotic. Indeed, without thorough training and firm discipline, they can just as easily disrupt your life as enrich it.

The Cats' Guide to People takes a comprehensive look at these unpredictable creatures, giving advice on essential topics such as selection, behaviour, health care, training techniques and people management.

Whether you already own humans, or are considering adopting some for the first time, this unique and informative study will help you understand and get the best from those you finally choose as your own.

POST A LITTLE HAPPINESS

Post·A·Book

A Royal Mail service in association with the Book Marketing Council & The Booksellers Association.

Post-A-Book is a Post Office trademark.

Book Tokens

Give them the pleasure of choosing

Book Tokens can be bought and exchanged at most bookshops in Great Britain and Ireland.

NEL BESTSELLERS

T51277	'THE NUMBER OF THE BEAST'	Robert Heinlein	£2.25
T50277	STRANGER IN A STRANGE LAND		
		Robert Heinlein	£1.75
T51382	FAIR WARNING	Simpson & Burger	£1.75
T52478	CAPTAIN BLOOD	Michael Blodgett	£1.75
T50246	THE TOP OF THE HILL	Irwin Shaw	£1.95
T49620	RICH MAN, POOR MAN	Irwin Shaw	£1.60
T51609	MAYDAY	Thomas Block	£1.75
T54071	MATCHING PAIR	George G. Gilman	£1.50
T45773	CLAIRE RAYNER'S LIFEGUIDE		£2.50
T53709	PUBLIC MURDERS	Bill Granger	£1.75
T53679	THE PREGNANT WOMAN'S		
	BEAUTY BOOK	Gloria Natale	£1.25
T49817	MEMORIES OF ANOTHER DAY	Harold Robbins	£1.95
T50807	79 PARK AVENUE	Harold Robbins	£1.75
T50149	THE INHERITORS	Harold Robbins	£1.75
T53231	THE DARK	James Herbert	£1.50
T43245	THE FOG	James Herbert	£1.50
T53296	THE RATS	James Herbert	£1.50
T45528	THE STAND	Stephen King	£1.75
T50874	CARRIE	Stephen King	£1.50
T51722	DUNE	Frank Herbert	£1.75
T51552	DEVIL'S GUARD	Robert Elford	£1.50
T52575	THE MIXED BLESSING	Helen Van Slyke	£1.75
T38602	THE APOCALYPSE	Jeffrey Konvitz	95p

NEL P.O. BOX 11, FALMOUTH TR10 9EN, CORNWALL

Postage Charge:
U.K. Customers 45p for the first book plus 20p for the second book and 14p for each additional book ordered to a maximum charge of £1.63.

B.F.P.O. & EIRE Customers 45p for the first book plus 20p for the second book and 14p for the next 7 books; thereafter 8p per book.

Overseas Customers 75p for the first book and 21p per copy for each additional book.

Please send cheque or postal order (no currency).

Name..

Address ....

....

Title...

While every effort is made to keep prices steady, it is sometimes necessary to increase prices at short notice. New English Library reserve the right to show on covers and charge new retail prices which may differ from those advertised in the text or elsewhere.(7)